IMPROVE THE POWER OF YOUR SUBCONSCIOUS MIND WITH SELF-HYPNOSIS

Use Positive Thinking to Change your Life

CHRISTIAN H. GODEFROY
DON R. STEEVENS

Club Positif

Copyright © 2017 by Club Positif

Copyright © 1991 by Christian H. Godefroy

All rights reserved.

No part of this book may be reproduced in any form or by any electronic or mechanical means, including information storage and retrieval systems, without written permission from the author, except for the use of brief quotations in a book review.

CONTENTS

Introduction	ix
1. THE HIDDEN POWERS OF YOUR MIND	1
Changing Yourself and Feeling Secure	3
Will the Method Work for You?	4
Hypnosis is a Natural State of Consciousness	5
The Extraordinary Power of the Subconscious	5
The Subconscious is Stronger because You Are Not Aware of Its Effects	7
Much of Our Subconscious 'Programming' Dates Back to Childhood	9
How Our Subconscious Works	9
Change Your Program and Change Your Life	11
How Are You Programmed?	13
How to Make Your Subconscious Work for You	16
The Power of Words	16
The Subconscious is a Powerful Amplifier	18
The Vital Importance of What You Tell Yourself	20
Stop Casting 'Evil Spells'	21
Exercise	22
How to Protect Yourself Against Harmful Exterior Influences	23
How to Defend Yourself Against Negative Suggestions	23
A Few Words Can Change Your Life	24
1. Formulate Your Suggestion in as Positive a Way as Possible	25
Which Verb Tense is Best for Formulations?	26
2. Formulate Your Suggestions in a Progressive Manner	26
3. Keep Your Formulations Brief	28
4. Use Simple, Clear Words	28
5. Is First or Second Person Better for Formulations?	28

Developing Your Suggestions	29
How Many Suggestions Can You Make at the Same Time?	29
Summary	30
The Golden Rule of Suggestion	31
How to Set Up a 'Dialogue' with Your Subconscious	32
The Immense Wisdom Lying Dormant Within You	33
How to Make a Difficult Decision	34
How to Question Your Subconscious	36
Your Subconscious is Especially Sensitive to the Language of Emotion	37
A Powerful Weapon for Good or Evil	38
How to React When You Have Negative Thoughts or Feelings	41
Exceeding Your Limitations	41
The Power of Images	43
The Amazing Power of Your Imagination	45
The Secret of Images	46
Your Imagination: a Personal Treasure Chest	47
The Power of the Law of Attraction	49
Create Your Luck	52
The Blackboard Technique	53
Be Attentive to Your Mental Images	54
SUMMARY OF CHAPTER 1	55
2. HOW TO INDUCE THE STATE OF SELF-HYPNOSIS	57
Relaxation	57
When is the Ideal Time for a Session of Self-Hypnosis?	58
An Emergency Session	59
A Few Minutes Can Change Your Life	60
How to Pack Two Days into One	61
Ideal Conditions for Self-hypnosis	62
To Relax- Breathe!	63
Try this Exercise	65
The Importance of Relaxation	67
Differential Relaxation	69
Concentrated Relaxation	74
Practical Procedure	76

Modern Science Makes a New Discovery about Relaxation	78
The Method: Your Passport to Total Happiness!	79
How to Come Out of the State of Self-hypnosis	83
How to Intensify Your Self-hypnosis Sessions	84
What to Do if It Doesn't Work	87
Create Your Own Method	88
SUMMARY OF CHAPTER 2	94
3. HOW TO UNBLOCK YOUR REAL PERSONALITY	**97**
Become a Winner!	99
How to Overcome an Inferiority Complex	100
Develop Your Self-confidence	101
Change Your Image Bank	102
How to Create a New Personality	104
How to Influence Others and Become a Leader	106
SUMMARY OF CHAPTER 3	111
4. GET HEALTHY AND STAY HEALTHY	**113**
How to Overcome Disease	114
The real origin of disease is in the mind	116
How a Suggestion Killed a Man	116
How We Program Ourselves to Be Ill	118
The Great Secret of Self-healing	119
Get Rid of Disease Through the Power of Your Mind	120
How to React in Order to Get Rid of an Illness Right from the Start	122
Healing Images	124
The Sun Technique	125
Emile Coué's Healing Method	125
How to Combat Nervous Fatigue and Overcome Insomnia	126
How to Get Rid of Pain at Will	129
Toothache	130
Substitution Technique for Dealing With Pain	130
How to Ease an Attack of Acute Arthritis	131
Beautiful Skin	131
Creative Visualization Exercise	132

Eliminate Migraines	132
Visual Variation	133
Digest Your Food With Ease	133
Why Can't People Get Rid of Their Allergies?	134
Verbal/Visual Healing Method	135
General Method	136
How to Overcome Asthma	136
How to Relieve Backaches	137
Help for a Stiff Neck	138
Overcoming Seasickness	138
Colds and Sinusitis	138
Heart Problems	139
SUMMARY OF CHAPTER 4	140
5. CONTROLLING YOUR HABITS AND ADDICTIONS	**143**
A Direct Effort of Will is Useless	143
Control Your Weight Without Depriving Yourself	144
Why Do All These Miracle Diets Fail?	145
Rules to Observe	146
A Mental Image You Can Use for Support	148
Stop Smoking in Two Weeks	148
How to Overcome Depression and Regain Your Love of Life	150
Some Important Advice	155
Visual Variation	157
The 'Positive Friend' Variation	157
Master Your Emotions	158
Visual Variation	160
How to Overcome Certain Other Habits	160
It's Easy to Stop Drinking	160
The 'Good Friend' Variation	162
Stop Biting Your Nails!	162
Overcoming Laziness and Messiness	162
Put an End to Bedwetting!	163
Phobias and Fears	164
SUMMARY OF CHAPTER 5	165
6. HOW TO IMPROVE YOUR LOVE LIFE	**167**
Overcoming Your Fear of the Opposite Sex	167

Visual Variation	169
How to Live as a Successful Couple and Make Love Grow	170
How to Overcome Impotence	172
Visual Variation	174
Frigidity Need No Longer Be a Problem	174
Visual Variation	175
How to Awaken Desire	176
SUMMARY OF CHAPTER 6	177

7. **HOW TO DEVELOP YOUR MEMORY, CREATIVITY AND SPORTING ABILITY** — 179

The Secret of an Efficient Memory	179
The Many Advantages of Having a Great Memory	181
The 'Friend' Technique	182
Visual Variation	183
Learn While You Sleep!	184
Concentration: the Key to Success	184
An Incredibly Powerful Exercise	187
How to Be Creative and Inspired	188
Inspiration Can Be Programmed	189
How to Develop Your Athletic Ability	190
Infallible Methods for Improving your Athletic Ability	192
SUMMARY OF CHAPTER 7	194

8. **CHOOSING SUCCESS, NOT FAILURE** — 195

Learn to Motivate Yourself for Success	195
How to Have as Much Money as You Want	198
How to Stay Young and Live Longer	199
Learn to Enjoy Life	201
SUMMARY OF CHAPTER 8	201
You can do anything	203
Appendix	205
Also by Christian H. Godefroy	207

INTRODUCTION

WHAT THIS BOOK CAN DO FOR YOU

Just imagine: for only a few dollars or pounds - the price of this book - you can acquire the key to so many of the good things in life which you may have thought were never going to come your way. Professional success, social poise, good health and so much more really can be yours.

Sounds too good to be true? Don't be cynical: it has worked for me, and for thousands of others. And the wonderful part is that you won't be at the mercy of doctors and analysts, drugs or therapy groups - you will be totally in control of all these exciting changes through the power of your own will and imagination.

What you are now holding in your hands, therefore, is the most precious tool imaginable for your personal development and success.

But as long as this tool stays on your bookshelf, it will do nothing for you. Read it once, then read it again, and make it work for you.

INTRODUCTION

Please try not to skip directly to Chapter 2, which explains how to hypnotize yourself. Keep reading the first chapter until you have understood it perfectly. It may seem long, but it is essential if you want to make the best use of this technique.

But what can it really do for me? you may be saying. Most of us have some corner of our lives in which we feel we have failed -maybe because we have never tried, having been programmed as children to believe we would not succeed.

This book will show you how easy it is to change all this, to become more effective and confident; in other words to alter your self-image.

If you sincerely believe that you have a terrific personality, everyone else will too. Yesterday's shrinking violet will shine at today's office meeting and soon be en route for promotion. The compulsive worrier will start looking beyond himself or herself and get interested in other people: a new, full social life will surely follow.

People who are regularly ill will discover how to reject the concept of illness through the power of positive thinking: a healthy, energetic, enjoyable lifestyle will soon be theirs for the taking. And in so many other fields - losing weight, giving up smoking, developing an excellent memory, possessing the power to influence others, improving your personal relationships and sex life, to name but a few - the safe, gentle science of self-hypnosis will achieve permanent, positive results.

The book has been written in a lively, conversational style to influence your subconscious more easily. The idea of writing it occurred to me during a session of self-hypnosis, and many of the chapters were transcribed directly on to tape during subsequent sessions. D. R. Steevens, my co-author, is one of the world's best- known specialists in the field of self-hypnosis. He has shared much of his expertise with me, and has reviewed every chapter, adding his own points and giving practical

INTRODUCTION

advice. I believe I can say, without boasting, that this book is the best ever written on the subject.

If you want to tackle a specific problem you may have, study Chapters 1 and 2 and then go directly to the chapter that is of special interest to you. However, it is preferable to read all the chapters, even if you only intend to concentrate on the first two and the one that is particularly relevant to you. Just see how powerful your subconscious mind can be!

I hope that you will be as enthusiastic as I am about this technique and what it can do for you. The possibilities are infinite - the only limitation is your own imagination. So now, get ready for a very special voyage. Fasten your seat belts, as we take off for health, happiness and success!

Christian H. Godefroy

THE HIDDEN POWERS OF YOUR MIND

Since the dawn of time, philosophers and wise men have been saying that people are asleep, and that they must be awakened. Through the power of your subconscious mind you can achieve this awakening. The technique you will learn to access the subconscious is self-hypnosis. It is probably the simplest and fastest way to attain your goals in life and to make full use of your potential.

The simplest way to define self-hypnosis starts with an explanation of hypnosis itself. The word is derived from the Greek hypnos, which originally referred to the god of sleep. It is true that the hypnotic state appears to resemble that of sleep, but the comparison stops there. In fact, a subject under hypnosis only seems to be sleeping to an outside observer.

The main difference between the two states is that hypnotized subjects remain lucid and aware of everything that is going on around them. Their perceptions are even sharper than during the normal waking state, but these perceptions are of another order.

To some extent, the state of hypnosis resembles that of a waking dream.

Willpower and thought take a back seat to imagination and the free association of ideas. Subjects relax more and more deeply, both physically and mentally. They may even experience a kind of euphoria.

And since they are immobile, their minds are no longer influenced by physical sensations, so that they can concentrate completely on precise thoughts or sensations. But above all, and of capital importance to the hypnotic state (also called the 'alpha' state and characterized by a significant slow-down in the emission of brain waves), subjects attain a high level of suggestibility.

What do we mean by suggestibility? Simply this: suggestibility is the capacity of the subconscious mind to receive suggestions from the conscious mind - suggestions which are oriented and pre-established in accordance with the subject's desires. It is important to understand this point clearly, since self-hypnosis is nothing more than a technique which allows us to access our subconscious at will.

Then we can free its enormous power and delve into its amazing storehouse of knowledge, so that it works for us and not against us (as is unfortunately the case for most people).

It is a well-known fact that most people only use about 10 per cent of their brain.

Some researchers have even suggested that 10 per cent is too high, and that the figure is closer to 4 per cent. Self-hypnosis allows you to tap into a substantially increased proportion of your brain, placing its hidden powers at your service.

You'll see just how simple it is as you read the book. I have perfected my method over the years, ceaselessly improving it thanks to the comments and observations of the people whom I have taught. In fact, it is so simple that we could go so far as to say that any individual who can read can transform his or her life with self-hypnosis.

In only a few days, you will feel the beginnings of the spectacular transformation about to take place in you - a transformation that you may have been awaiting for far too long. The time has finally come for you to take charge of your own destiny and to start controlling circumstances, instead of being a victim.

Practice the exercises for a few minutes a day, and after only a few weeks you won't recognize yourself. You'll have become another person - the person you probably always dreamed of being. You'll be more fulfilled, happier, loved and admired by the people around you, and firmly grasping the reins of your own destiny. Isn't that what every man and woman dreams of achieving, and rightly so?

CHANGING YOURSELF AND FEELING SECURE

Let's take another look at the initial distinction we made between hypnosis and self-hypnosis. Hypnosis requires a hypnotist and a subject. The hypnotist directs all the operations, while the subject passively submits to the hypnotist's directions and suggestions.

Note, however, that subjects must generally be consenting for the hypnotic state to take effect, and, contrary to what many people believe, will do nothing that goes against their better moral judgment. Cheap literature and sensational films have propagated a false conception of hypnotism as something dangerous and even demonic-rest assured, this has no basis of truth whatsoever.

In any case - and this is the great advantage of my method -people who practice self-hypnosis are never at the mercy of a possibly unscrupulous or incompetent hypnotist, since they themselves play this role. They can therefore feel completely secure. In addition, the method is, for that very reason, more accessible and much less costly.

You are alone, working with yourself, with the deepest and also the most powerful part of your personality, the very center of your being. You don't have to disclose your problems to anyone else. You have to confront only yourself - the obstacles you wish to overcome or the negative habits you wish to change. What could be better than that?

WILL THE METHOD WORK FOR YOU?

Some people are skeptical about self-hypnosis and think that only weak-minded or weak-willed persons can be hypnotized. Nothing is further from the truth. In fact, experiments - and not only my own, but also those of numerous doctors, psychologists and therapists- have demonstrated the opposite. Many great and very strong-willed persons such as Henry Ford, Thomas Edison and a host of famous artists and writers have used self-hypnosis to achieve their goals. Anyone, no matter what his or her present level of achievement, can successfully practice self- hypnosis with no danger whatsoever.

What's more, you have already been hypnotized without knowing it. When you get absorbed in a fascinating book or film, or listen to music, or lose all sense of time as you concentrate on a particular task, or are swept off your feet by an especially powerful and charismatic speaker- and later describe the speech as 'hypnotic' - you are actually in a kind of hypnotic state. So you can see that it happens quite naturally, and that the fears we entertain concerning hypnosis are completely unwarranted.

HYPNOSIS IS A NATURAL STATE OF CONSCIOUSNESS

The only thing we need to guard against is deliberately trying to use self- hypnosis for negative reasons, which will ultimately hurt only ourselves. As you will appreciate after reading further, the power of hypnosis or self-hypnosis has a permanent effect on our lives. The problem is that in most cases, and without our being aware of it, this force is working against us. It is therefore fortunate that you are reading these lines today, and not next year or in ten years' time because, even if the only thing you get out of this book is an understanding of this fact, it will make all my years of work on this method worthwhile. The point is - and we'll be talking about this a lot in the following pages - your life is an exact mirror of your thoughts.

To summarize, then, self-hypnosis is the simplest and most effective modern method for accessing the mind's subconscious and making use of its prodigious powers.

THE EXTRAORDINARY POWER OF THE SUBCONSCIOUS

What exactly is this subconscious that we hear so much about? There are several definitions, not all of them clear-cut. Since the method described in this book is essentially practical, we will not enter into any long theoretical or historical discussions.

It is enough to say that the concept of the subconscious (also called unconscious) mind was initially explored by Sigmund Freud, who made it the cornerstone of his entire system of psychiatry and saw it as the source of most human behavior, especially that behavior which we believe to be purely voluntary. Freud's contri- bution to understanding our behavior and its true nature is therefore considerable, despite certain exaggerations he may have made.

One thing is certain: even if the theorists cannot agree on a single definition of the exact nature of the subconscious, the fact that it exists cannot be doubted, and it has been accepted by the scientific community for many years.

To put it simply, the human mind is divided into two parts: one is conscious, and the other unconscious. The conscious part, which is only active during waking hours, takes care of most routine and intellectual activities.

When you eat or pour yourself a drink, or work on your monthly budget or fill out your tax return (forgetting to do these things, as you will see later on, is often due to your subconscious dictating what seems to be an involuntary act), it is your conscious mind which is being brought into play. As for your subconscious, it takes care of all your vital functions. For example, you don't have to think about breathing in order to breathe. If you did, you'd have serious problems sleeping!

Your subconscious also records and stores everything that happens in your life, like an archive of your entire existence. Its memory is perfect: it forgets nothing. It is also your subconscious which makes you fall in love with one person and not with another. Your conscious mind may advise you against such a choice: a particular man or woman may not appear to have the necessary qualities to merit your love. Yet your subconscious is stronger, and you are irresistibly attracted towards that person, despite the fact that he or she may not appear to be the ideal candidate.

Here's another example, this time more obvious. You want to stop smoking. You really want to stop - or at least you try to convince yourself that you do. And yet you can't stop. This is because your subconscious, which among other things is the cause of all your habits - good and bad - won't let you stop. It has been programmed to think differently. Later on I'll be talking a lot more about this extremely important notion of programming.

You walk into a supermarket and, spontaneously and mechanically - in fact just like a robot or a puppet - you 'choose' one brand of soap powder. Once again you are being guided by your subconscious, simply because it has been programmed, without your being aware of it, by some advertisement which struck your fancy (and in fact the methods used in marketing are strikingly similar to those of hypnosis).

THE SUBCONSCIOUS IS STRONGER BECAUSE YOU ARE NOT AWARE OF ITS EFFECTS

Thousands of examples could be provided of how the subconscious affects behavior. And some have a much more dramatic and important effect than the kind already mentioned. Did you know, for example, that when a person fails repeatedly at a task, despite being talented and hard working, it is because of his or her subconscious mind? Did you know that the same goes for emotional failures? Did you know that most illnesses - some doctors even suggest all illnesses - arise and first develop in your subconscious mind? Does that surprise you?

Let's look at another example, one that we've all seen thousands of times. A woman seems to have everything going for her. Nature endowed her with physical beauty, she has an interesting and well-paid job, she seems to be happily married, with a circle of good friends, is able to take a month's holiday every year - and yet, inexplicably, she is unhappy. She may even be considering suicide. She gets more and more depressed. She feels as though she's about to have a nervous breakdown.

The worst thing is that, although she can confide in people close to her, no one believes her. They think she's making it up, that she's looking for pity. How can someone have so much and dare to pretend to be unhappy?

And yet this woman is not lying. She is telling the absolute truth when she describes her state of mind. The real reason is that her subconscious is stronger than her conscious mind. At some point in her life it must have received some very negative programming, which has been reinforced over time. The subconscious is always stronger and always has the last word, which is why reprogramming your subconscious - positively - can achieve such wonderful results.

Many proverbs say the same thing, for example: 'Happiness is a state of mind.' In this sense- and up to a certain point- external circumstances are not a determining factor. Thus two persons, when placed in similar situations and confronted with the same kinds of obstacles, may react completely differently. One may do what is required without getting too emotional or 'losing their cool', while the other gets totally flustered and depressed. It is, therefore, the person's state of mind- their mental predisposition - which is the determining factor in how he or she may cope.

I hope these few examples have convinced you of the extraordinary power of the subconscious. Our conscious mind has often been compared to the tip of an iceberg. As you probably know, the proportion of the iceberg which is under water, and therefore invisible, is far larger than the part you can see. The same goes for the subconscious (or unconscious).

This image provides an accurate picture of the relative powers of the two parts of our mind. The subconscious is much more powerful, even if people believe they are very strong-willed. It is only after becoming aware of the power of the subconscious that you can start forging your own destiny and transforming your life into how you want it.

MUCH OF OUR SUBCONSCIOUS 'PROGRAMMING' DATES BACK TO CHILDHOOD

For the famous seventeenth-century French philosopher René Descartes, the greatest unhappiness was having been a child. It wasn't because he didn't like children – he was a father himself–but because during childhood, the mind accepts all kinds of prejudiced opinions, beliefs and suggestions without question. It took him years to get rid of these prejudices, which he did by applying his own system of 'rational doubt'.

We are programmed by our parents, often without their knowing it.

Unfortunately, they often do so in a negative way. A child's subconscious is so impressionable that ideas are engraved on it like a stylus digging into soft wax. It generally takes years for people to become aware of their own programming and, if necessary, to undo the negative impressions which were inscribed in their subconscious when they were children.

Fortunately, we can use self-hypnosis first to erase the negative programs from our minds, and later to reprogram ourselves according to our desires and aspirations. Self-hypnosis can help us to cleanse ourselves of all our negative habits and tendencies, of an apparently predetermined 'fate', which is in fact the result of subconscious images and processes that we can change.

HOW OUR SUBCONSCIOUS WORKS

I have just compared the subconscious to soft wax in order to show how impressionable it is. The most striking and illuminating comparison is without a doubt the one made by Dr Maxwell Maltz, author of the international bestseller Psycho-Cybernetics. Once you have read my book, I recommend Dr Maltz's as a means of enhancing your understanding of the subconscious.

This world-famous cosmetic surgeon (who developed his theory after realizing that even radical modifications to the face and/ or other parts of the body were not enough to change people's self-image) compared the subconscious to a computer.

And when you talk about computers, you have to talk about programming. So the first point in the comparison is that the subconscious is programmed just like a computer- and, indeed, I have used this term on one or two occasions already.

The second point is that a computer, like the subconscious, is immensely powerful. Its capabilities are generally much superior to those of the operator in terms of the number of functions it can perform and the rapidity with which it can perform them.

The third point of comparison is that computers, like the subconscious, possess a perfect and implacable kind of logic. Enter a certain type of program, say for example one that I use a lot, which involves checking a list of names for potential clients who meet certain criteria, and the computer will go about its task and find the names you are looking for. But it will not find anything else. Its program - its mandate - stops there. The subconscious acts in the same way. Like a computer, it accepts any suggestion or program uncritically and executes it blindly.

Paradoxically, the subconscious is infinitely wise and infinitely powerful, but at the same time it does not, so to speak, have any free will. The same goes for computers. Without a program, a computer can't do anything. The subconscious can't do anything without a program either.

However, it is absolutely impossible for the subconscious not to be programmed.

The most reliable studies have shown that even in the womb the fetus's sub-conscious is already registering impressions (for example, feeling the mother's anxiety), which many years after birth can be recalled during deep hypnosis.

On a number of occasions I have witnessed amazing regressions in which the subject relived moments experienced while still in the womb. All this provides yet more proof that the subconscious records absolutely everything.

The subconscious is reactive, in the sense that it can only respond to an impulse or a program or a command that is given to it. The programs which determine how it functions come from either the person himself or herself, or from outside. The second category includes parents, friends and society in general.

Unfortunately, most people have been receiving negative programming for a very long time - normally without realizing that they have been programmed at all.

They think they can do nothing to change their lives, that 'they are who they are' and must simply submit to events and circumstances, accepting that there are many more low points in life than high points. Such pessimism is widespread, and fits perfectly into a system which behaviorists call 'positive reinforcement' (although there may be nothing positive about it!).

CHANGE YOUR PROGRAM AND CHANGE YOUR LIFE

The simple fact of being aware of this extremely important truth about your mind and your life places you in a class apart. You now have a foot in the door, and will soon be able to enter fully into life - real life, a new life, a life of exceptional fulfillment. It's up to you, and you alone.

Think about this concept of the inevitable programming of all beings; it's not easy to grasp its profound meaning all at once.

Have you ever asked yourself what the real reasons are for acting in a certain way in a given situation - especially if your actions are negative?

Why, for example, do you always come up with the perfect response to someone you are trying to impress - but not until hours or days afterwards? Or why don't you get the pay rise you deserve while colleagues, despite being less gifted or less loyal, seem to climb the career ladder with disturbing ease, regularly receiving substantial salary increases? You don't think it's fair. Or at least, that's what you consciously think.

But delve a little deeper into the problem. After all, you only have to be frank with yourself- no one else has to know what you genuinely think. In fact, sincerity - being honest with yourself- is the springboard for all progress. When you really think about it, isn't it possible that something deep down inside you believes you don't deserve a rise? That you don't have the right to ask for one, even though your rational, conscious mind may be telling you that your request is perfectly legitimate?

Maybe something happened during your childhood, maybe your parents or a teacher or a friend ridiculed your first spontaneous attempts to assert yourself; perhaps they told you that you were incapable, that you had to stop dreaming and face up to reality ....

How sad these kinds of criticism are; even sadder are the lives they ruin. Of course, the people who programmed them into you may not have been deliberately trying to harm you. They were simply not aware of the powerful effect that such criticism can have on impressionable young minds. Such critics continually create negative effects in the people around them - but without knowing it. In this way, a cycle, which we could call a 'chain of unhappiness', is set up. The good news is that you can break the chain, not only for yourself but also for the people around you.

When you begin to work your way out of this situation through my technique of self-hypnosis, you will soon become aware of your beneficial influence on the people around you. People will be attracted to you because of your uniqueness, your originality. And that's because, these days, the sad fact is that the most original thing you can be is happy-happy and positive. You will attract people like a magnet. Your personality will exude power and charisma. People will seek you out, like travelers searching for an oasis in the desert.

HOW ARE YOU PROGRAMMED?

Now is the time to stop reading for a short while and do some self-analysis, to discover how you are programmed at the moment. In general, programs can be categorized as positive or negative. Ask yourself sincerely which category you fall into.

If you suffer from fatigue and apathy when you wake up in the morning, if you rely on alcohol to solve your problems or are depressed, if you are dissatisfied with your relationships or have serious sexual problems, if you are ill more often than you should be, if you are apathetic and lack direction... in all likelihood you have a negative program.

If, on the other hand, life is like a game to you (a game which may present occasional problems, but which you nevertheless find extremely pleasurable); if you are overflowing with energy, if you like your work, if your health is good, if you are always getting involved in new projects, if other people seem spontaneously drawn to you, if you earn enough money and your occasional financial problems are only temporary, if you are in a happy relationship, if you quickly recover from setbacks or failures, if you are motivated by a love of life... than you belong to that group of people whom the nineteenth-century French novelist Stendhal referred to as 'the happy few' - the elect, the very small number of positive people.

You will probably fall somewhere between the two.

If, on the whole, you are more positive than negative (which is likely to be the case, since most positive people are continually trying to improve themselves by surrounding themselves with positive people and by reading books, such as this one, on motivation and personal development), well ... all the better. My method will be useful to you in two ways.

First, it will benefit others, since you will learn a simple scientific way to program the people around you - your partner, your colleagues, your friends, your children and so on.

And secondly it will be of benefit to you personally, since although you may be a positive person in general, everyone has their dark, negative side, their secret, unfulfilled desires. There are always facets of our character that can be improved.

You may be a generally good-natured person, let's say, but you just can't seem to kick the smoking habit, which poisons your surroundings and poses a risk to your health. You may be paid a decent salary, but you'd like to know how to earn more.

Maybe you just feel you want more out of life. There's nothing wrong with that - it's a perfectly legitimate desire. And I can assure you that my technique will help fulfill that desire, and even exceed your expectations.

If, however, you are more negative than positive, you have in fact just taken a decisive step- by realizing it, and admitting it (if only to yourself). But don't worry; it's not that serious. Any program, even one that is deeply ingrained, can be modified or erased. Later on I'll show you how to deprogram and then reprogram yourself in order to transform your personality. And the step you've already taken- self-analysis- is the first, decisive step in the process of reprogramming. You have already identified your weaknesses and your unfulfilled desires. However, you must understand what I mean by the word 'identify'.

I'm not talking about some kind of psychoanalysis - in other words, I haven't asked you to identify the causes of your negative programming. These causes are often obscure, buried in the distant memories of childhood or hidden in the deepest recesses of your subconscious. Psychoanalysis has made an important contribution to a theoretical understanding of the human mind-and I do mean theoretical, since the practical results achieved by even the greatest practitioners are much less impressive. Psychoanalytical treatment is usually long and expensive, and cannot guarantee results; in fact a member of psychoanalysts attribute apparent cures to the factor of time itself- as if patients have, in a manner of speaking, 'served their time'.

Let me try to illustrate the difference between self-hypnosis and psychoanalysis.

Your mind or personality is like a car. The car breaks down, and you don't know a thing about what happens under the bonnet. So you get your car towed to a garage.

The driver of the towing vehicle may be able to explain what the problem is, but he doesn't actually repair the car. He's like a psychoanalyst. To get the car fixed you have to wait for a mechanic to open the bonnet and repair or replace the faulty parts. The mechanic may tell you later on what the cause of the problem was, in order to justify the bill. But the important thing is that the car is fixed and you can keep on driving. That is what self-hypnosis does. It is practical.

HOW TO MAKE YOUR SUBCONSCIOUS WORK FOR YOU

The subconscious is governed by the laws of cause and effect, just like the rest of the physical world in which we live. Every thought is an action. In fact, each thought is a cause, which produces exterior effects. There's nothing astonishing about that, when you think about it. Isn't it true that thought rules the world? In fact, behind every act and every invention known to man, there first lies a thought.

Even before doing something as commonplace as moving a chair, you have to think about it. Some actions are mechanical, you say, and don't require any thought. I agree. Nevertheless, the first time you performed that action, before it became mechanical, you did have to think about it.

The subconscious is like a fertile field. If you plant a field with carrot seeds in the spring, you shouldn't be surprised to find yourself harvesting carrots in the autumn. This law of cause and effect is just as valid for the subconscious.

Therefore, to make your subconscious work properly for you, you have to start planting the seeds of positive thoughts today: thoughts of happiness and success, love and peace - and, of course, health.

You have to install a completely new program in yourself. Remember: as soon as an idea is accepted by the subconscious, it is put to use. That sounds simple enough. But how can you create a positive program? That's what we'll be looking at in the next section. And it is very simple, as you'll see.

THE POWER OF WORDS

You get to your office in the morning, already on edge because of the problems awaiting you, and a little fuzzy because you were out late having a good time the night before (perfectly acceptable, since it was your birthday). The only breakfast you had time for was a fast cup of coffee. Nevertheless, you feel pretty good. A little less alert than usual, perhaps, but if the only thing that mattered was staying in shape, you wouldn't be able to have any fun, right?

A colleague greets you, smiling at first, but then the smile fades and, with a worried expression, he asks you if you're feeling all right. You hasten to reassure him that yes, you're fine, you were just out late, it's nothing serious .... 'You should get some rest,' the colleague insists. You remember that you don't really like this person at all.

'Why doesn't he mind his own business?' you think. 'After all, he looks like a corpse himself most of the time.'

As you're walking down the passage to your office, another colleague stops you and, with a worried expression, asks, 'Are you ill? Have you got flu or something?' 'No, no, just a touch of indigestion. Nothing serious .... ' So now you've switched stories. It isn't your night out any more, it's indigestion. You are gradually succumbing to the suggestions being made to you. You're losing ground. And if you happen to run into a third person who makes a similar remark about the way you look, you'll soon find you don't feel at all well. You'll stop in front of the first mirror you see, and examine yourself. Yes, it's true you don't look so good. Maybe you're getting a cold. Or perhaps it's that stomach ulcer acting up again, the one you thought was completely cured. Is that pain you feel in your stomach?

As the morning progresses, the phone rings constantly, more and more problems arise, and by eleven o'clock you find that you're not feeling well at all. You decide to go home after lunch and lie down for a while to get a little rest. You must be coming down with that cold.

This scenario may be commonplace, but it contains an important lesson. You've surely experienced a similar situation in your own life, a situation where you fall victim to a verbal suggestion. Your subconscious accepts an external suggestion, which it internalizes, and which then results in your really feeling ill, even though to begin with you did not feel ill at all.

THE SUBCONSCIOUS IS A POWERFUL AMPLIFIER

You have already fallen victim to the prodigious power of words. It happens all the time. Say someone calls you a liar in public. Even if the accusation is completely untrue (and unless you have developed the inner strength to remain indifferent to negative suggestions), the chances are that you will get angry or at least feel insulted. And yet, if you think about it, you have to admit that it's only words that are making you so upset - words which do not even describe reality.

This is because the subconscious does not differentiate between ideas that are true and those that are false. Later on I shall be talking more about this very important point, which is actually a corollary to the idea that the subconscious is like a fertile field.

But now let's look at some more examples of the formidable power of words.

Someone says they love you. If you find that person attractive, your heart starts beating faster and you become excited and aroused. And yet, what you are reacting to are only words. The person may be sincere, or may only be out to have some fun- to tease you. However, your subconscious accepts the suggestion without question and immediately translates it into visible, easily understandable signs.

Let's consider a second example: Your boss congratulates you on the work you've been doing. Although he (or she) may not believe a word of what he's saying, it still makes you feel great. Your confidence shoots up, and you attack your work with added enthusiasm (which may have been your boss's aim in the first place!).

The third example - a true story, by the way - is much more dramatic. A doctor informed a patient who had come in for a routine examination that he was suffering from an incurable disease and had only a few months left to live. Of course the patient was stunned. How could the simple tests the doctor performed have led to such a drastic prognosis? The patient felt fine when he walked into the doctor's surgery. Nevertheless, his life underwent a complete transformation. He really did fall ill -seriously ill. He was soon close to death, and probably would have died had he not been informed at the last minute that it was all a mistake - his file had been mixed up with that of another patient.

This anecdote proves once again that the subconscious will accept any kind of suggestion, even ones that are completely false, especially if the suggestion is first accepted by the conscious mind. In fact, if you think about the case I have just described, a man was almost killed by a simple word from his doctor; his subconscious did all the rest.

And this leads us to another fundamental characteristic of the subconscious mind.

It is an important one to understand if you are going to use the power of the subconscious to your advantage or if you want to be able to resist its influence in harmful situations. This characteristic is especially important in situations engendered by other people (and other people, even those who are close to us and pretend to love us, rarely exercise a wholly positive influence on our subconscious since they themselves often have a negative program, and are not aware of the effect their words have on the people around them).

The fundamental principle I am talking about is this: the subconscious acts like a magnifying glass- it enlarges everything it perceives. We have already seen to what degree the subconscious can exaggerate a suggestion, especially if it is regularly reinforced (fortunately it can go in either direction - positive or negative - depending on the suggestion). But we must remember that the subconscious is reactive, and accepts all suggestions blindly. The applications of this principle of amplification are infinite.

THE VITAL IMPORTANCE OF WHAT YOU TELL YOURSELF

For this reason, you have to be extremely careful about what kinds of thoughts you allow your mind to focus on during the day. People generally have an inner monologue going during most of their waking hours. Did you know that this seemingly innocent inner monologue exerts a profound influence on your life? You are ceaselessly sending suggestions to your subconscious, which in turn acts like a sponge, absorbing everything indiscriminately.

Now it's time for another brief period of self-analysis, which should prove to be very instructive. What kinds of things do you ordinarily think about?

Some people, doubtlessly without being aware of it, are continually repeating to themselves that things are going badly, that life is boring and difficult, that most people are detestable, that they are tired of it all, and so on. Before an important event such as a job interview or a first date this inner monologue accelerates, usually in a negative sense, revealing some kind of worry, which the subconscious immediately adopts and amplifies out of all proportion. In such situations, it is obvious that your subconscious is working against you. The consequences are often more extreme and problematical than the original situation. A singer may lose her voice on the opening night of a show, or an actor can forget his lines, or an otherwise well-qualified candidate can become completely flustered during an interview... the variations are infinite.

STOP CASTING 'EVIL SPELLS'

The power of words has been acknowledged since the dawn of history. Consider the importance of prayer in most religions. Oriental religions, for example, use a form of prayer called 'mantra', where a word, or group of words, endowed with some special meaning, is endlessly repeated. The results can be astonishing. The modern technique referred to as 'autosuggestion', used by many doctors the world over, consists of repeating a scientifically formulated word or phrase- much like a 'mantra'. Practitioners of magic also repeat certain formulas which they believe are endowed with magical properties. But on the whole there are only two kinds of formulas: those that are beneficial and those that are harmful.

Here is a list of harmful formula phrases (a little like evil spells cast on yourself by yourself), which you should avoid at all cost:

- I can't
- I shouldn't
- I'm going to fail
- I'm not lucky
- I'm always wrong
- It's not for me
- I'm already too old
- I've never been successful, so how can I be successful now?
- Nobody loves me
- I'm not a likeable person
- I can never seem to get my act together

- I'm going bankrupt
- I'm going to lose my job
- My wife/husband is going to leave me
- I'll always be unhappy
- I'm going to be ill
- I'm always tired
- I'm neurotic
- I'm shy
- I don't know how to assert myself in public
- Nobody pays any attention to me
- I'll never get very far in life
- I'm worthless
- Success isn't in the cards for me
- I was born under a bad sign
- I'll never change

The list could go on and on, but you'll have got the idea by now. You must always protect yourself against this kind of thinking and prevent such thoughts from reaching your subconscious. When someone looks at a project of yours and says, 'This will never work ....' you must not accept that opinion. If you do, your project is all but dead. Your confidence will begin to erode and the idea, brilliant though it may be, will probably abort before it gets off the ground. Your mind will be accepting the idea of failure, the thought will take hold, and eventually it will materialize in the circumstances of your life.

EXERCISE

Make a note of any other negative formulas you find yourself repeating. Update the list regularly.

HOW TO PROTECT YOURSELF AGAINST HARMFUL EXTERIOR INFLUENCES

You should not only be careful about the involuntary (and unfortunately often harmful) suggestions you continually make to yourself; you must also pay particular attention to suggestions coming from others. We have already looked at the kinds of disastrous consequences that exterior suggestions can have on people, but that is no reason to get discouraged. In all the cases described, each of the subjects consciously accepted the exterior, negative suggestion.

That is the root of the problem. Remember: a suggestion that is not accepted has absolutely no effect- it slides off like water off a duck's back. Refusing to accept a suggestion may sound easy, but it's a lot harder to do. Sometimes you just can't resist - it's stronger than you are. Or, as is more often the case, the negative suggestion does make some sense-we already have some doubts, fears, hesitations and so on, and these are nourished and reinforced by every new negative suggestion to which we are exposed.

HOW TO DEFEND YOURSELF AGAINST NEGATIVE SUGGESTIONS

I'm going to give you a powerful weapon with which to defend yourself. The first thing is to react quickly to any suggestion that you judge to be harmful. Better still, combine this with one of the fundamental principles of the mind, a process which is most effective in combating any harmful new influences trying to take hold, and which is also an ancient and almost instinctive part of your behavior - the principle of substitution.

When you, or someone else, try to plant a negative suggestion in your mind, you can successfully protect yourself by immediately replacing it with an opposite and positive suggestion. So if someone keeps telling you that you're going to fail, that you'll never be able to get out of the rut you're in, you can counterattack by telling yourself: 'I will succeed, my life is improving day by day...' and so on (we'll be studying exactly how to formulate positive suggestions in the next section).

Therefore, if you find yourself repeating thoughts like, 'I feel as if I'm going to be ill', the chances are that the suggestion will take root in your subconscious. Without discriminating, the subconscious will in turn start sending your body signals that it is getting ill. React immediately. Don't wait. Start making positive suggestions to yourself: 'I feel terrific - my health is improving daily. Tomorrow I'll wake up in great shape, completely rested and healthy...' and so on.

I cannot overemphasize the importance of this point. You have to be extremely attentive- obviously without becoming obsessive - to the flow of your own thoughts. The idea of getting ill, for example, usually permeates the subconscious in a very subtle way- By the time we become aware of it, it's usually too late: the illness has already established itself. You can help to fight it off by making further suggestions adapted for the purpose, but it would have been so much easier to do this earlier on when the idea of illness was still trying to take root in your mind.

So be on your guard. Become the guardian of your thoughts. Don't forget - you are what you think. To live a happy life, you have to think happy thoughts. This is a universal law, which appears to have no exceptions.

A FEW WORDS CAN CHANGE YOUR LIFE

Now you're going to learn how to use the power of words to your own advantage.

Positive formulation is an art, which follows certain rules; as you will see, they are simple to understand and apply.

An ideal suggestion has a number of characteristics, which I will enumerate in a moment (although there is probably no 'ideal' formula which works for everyone - you have to choose the type of suggestion which best suits your temperament, your background, your personality and so on). However, to be effective a formulation should meet certain requirements:

1. FORMULATE YOUR SUGGESTION IN AS POSITIVE A WAY AS POSSIBLE

This may seem obvious, since all we've been talking about for the last few pages has been positive suggestions. Let me explain. For a suggestion to become operative, and especially to prevent a suggestion from having an opposite effect to the one intended, it must express what we want to obtain, and not what we wish to avoid or correct.

So instead of saying, 'I don't have a stomach ulcer...' you have to make an affirmation like, 'My digestion is getting better all the time.' Instead of saying, 'I won't sleep late in the morning any more...' you should formulate the suggestion intended to correct your laziness as an affirmation, such as, 'I can now get up in the morning feeling great.' Instead of the negatively formulated suggestion, 'I don't have any more financial worries...' say, 'My financial situation is getting more secure every day.'

As we have seen, the subconscious is reactive: it reacts, but does not reason. For example, it is not equipped to decode all the nuances of a given formulation (although the conscious mind can easily do so) and essentially perceives only the dominating idea. In statements like, 'I don't have a stomach ulcer...' or, 'I don't have any financial worries...' what do you think the dominating ideas or key words are?

If the sentences are repeated very rapidly, or heard from a distance, 'stomach ulcer' and 'financial worries' are the phrases that will be retained. And that's how the subconscious records things. It does not account for negations.

WHICH VERB TENSE IS BEST FOR FORMULATIONS?

Some specialists recommend the present tense. Instead of saying something like, 'I will find a good job...' they suggest it's better to say, 'I now have a good job.' The problem is that this kind of present tense formulation often leads to a mental conflict, which discourages the subject. If you affirm that you are rich when actually you're poor as a church mouse, or that 'I am now slim...' when you're definitely overweight, your conscious mind will be faced with an inevitable contradiction. Consequently, the subconscious will tend to reject the suggestion or only partially accept it, making it much less effective.

So using the present tense presents certain problems. Here's how I suggest overcoming this difficulty.

2. FORMULATE YOUR SUGGESTIONS IN A PROGRESSIVE MANNER

This will avoid creating mental conflicts for your subconscious. Here are a few examples (as you will see, it's usually the verb which expresses the concept of progress).

- An insurance salesman is worried about his sluggish sales. Instead of saying, 'Sales are going well...', which his conscious mind would find hard to accept, he can say, 'Starting today, sales are improving day by day.' The sales may only go up 1 per cent on a given day, but there is still no contradiction in the formulation.
- Problems with obesity: 'I'm getting slimmer day by day...' or 'I am progressively reaching my ideal weight.'

- Problems with people: 'I'm becoming more and more positive towards people. People like me, and are spontaneously drawn to me...'
- Problems at work: 'My productivity is improving day by day. I find my work more and more fulfilling.'
- Memory problems: 'My memory is improving daily, and I can remember everything I need to in order to do my work.'

Another way of resolving the problem of tense in formulations, while still getting satisfactory results, is to exclude verbs altogether. People have witnessed spectacular improvements in their precarious financial situations after simply repeating the following words to themselves: 'SUCCESS - WEALTH'.

The advantage of these two miraculous words is that they are extremely simple, they imply no contradiction and they can be applied to almost any aspect of life.

We seek success everywhere, in all areas of our lives, in our relationships, in our careers and so on. And of course wealth does not only refer to material things: it can also be spiritual, artistic or emotional.

So why not start today and get into the habit of repeating these two simple words? They are an extremely powerful antidote for a host of problems. You can also use other pairs of words as formulations, depending on your needs:

HEALTH – RELAXATION
CONFIDENCE – CALM
LOVE - JOY

3. KEEP YOUR FORMULATIONS BRIEF

Formulations that are too long usually make less of an impression on your subconscious and are therefore less effective. The best formulations are usually the shortest. Also, if you've decided to do mental repetitions of your formulations (as we shall see later, there are a number of other options open to you, depending on your personality and taste), then memorizing brief ones is much easier.

4. USE SIMPLE, CLEAR WORDS

Choose words that you like and are familiar to you, words that make you feel at ease, words that don't provoke or shock you in any way.

5. IS FIRST OR SECOND PERSON BETTER FOR FORMULATIONS?

Should you use 'I' or 'you'? The choice is up to you. However, if you decide to tape your formulations 'you' is more effective. It's as if another person were talking to you, convincing you to assimilate the suggestions. The taped voice affirms that you are making progress, that you are improving, and constitutes a kind of conscience that watches over the way you think and the kinds of things you want.

Also, since a certain degree of passivity is helpful in getting the suggestions to work for you, using the pronoun 'you' is better since it implies an aspect of authority.

On the other hand, if you've opted for a mental repetition of the formulation, using the pronoun 'I' would be more natural. However, the best thing is to try both pronouns and see which works best for you.

DEVELOPING YOUR SUGGESTIONS

Write down your suggestions. Then try to develop them, improving them in the light of the principles you have just learnt. The simple fact of writing them down already constitutes a positive reinforcement, confirming your affirmation and your desire to make progress.

HOW MANY SUGGESTIONS CAN YOU MAKE AT THE SAME TIME?

Experience has demonstrated that it is infinitely more effective to make only one suggestion per session, and preferably one that is very specific. If you want to give up smoking, for instance, use the formulation provided in Chapter 5 or create one yourself. But only deal with one problem at a time.

This will avoid creating any confusion in your subconscious, and you'll start seeing results more rapidly. At first, when you are still unfamiliar with self- hypnosis, you should start working on problems that are easy to solve. You'll get rapid results, which will in turn encourage you and increase your confidence. And don't forget that each victory, however insignificant it may appear, will have a positive effect on your personality which is much more extensive than the simple result you have obtained. One small victory leads to another, larger one. The power of your mind will grow, and you will acquire the proof you need to believe that you can improve.

You may object to imposing these limitations on yourself, saying for example that, although you want to stop smoking, you'd also like to see some more general improvements in your life. And you're right - but let me explain. When I say that it's better not to work on two problems at the same time, I'm talking about specific problems, like trying to improve your memory simultaneously with trying to lose weight. Dealing with these two problems in the same session may well confuse your subconscious since, as explained earlier, the subconscious is in many ways just like a computer - and if you know anything about computers, you will know that you can't ask it to run two programs at the same time.

But it is quite reasonable to want to transform your life in general while still working on a particular problem. Here's what I suggest: use two formulations per session, one general and the other specific. Start with the general formulation, repeating or listening to it for a few minutes, and then move on to the second.

One of the best known general formulations is the one created by Emile Coué, a modest pharmacist from the French city of Nancy who transformed the lives of thousands of people. You may have heard about the formulation already, as a number of authors have quoted it or come up with variations. It is an ideal formulation as far as form is concerned - it meets all the requirements we have established:

Every day, in every way, I am getting better and better

The formulation is positive, progressive, brief, simple and has the great advantage of relating to all aspects of life. I've been using it for a number of years, and I can assure you that its powerful effects have not ceased to amaze me. So I can highly recommend it.

SUMMARY

1. Formulate your suggestions in as positive a way as possible.
2. Make your formulations progressive.
3. Keep your formulations brief.
4. Choose words that are simple and clear.
5. Use only one (specific) suggestion per session.

Exercise

Take all the negative suggestions you discovered in the previous exercise and replace them with positive formulations. In other words, find the antidotes for your negative thoughts.

THE GOLDEN RULE OF SUGGESTION

There's another rule you have to respect in order for a formulation to be successful.

The golden rule of suggestion is repetition

There's nothing surprising about that, when you stop to think. What do advertisers do when they want to introduce a new product, or increase demand for an existing one? They send out a constant barrage of publicity, inundating the public with their message.

You must do exactly the same thing when practicing self-hypnosis. Continually repeat the formulation you have chosen, thereby inundating your subconscious with its message.

When you ask someone for something, you don't always get it at the first attempt.

But if you ask again, and then again and again, the person's resistance will often wear down and you'll finally get what you want. The same goes for the subconscious. You have to communicate what you want it to do for you as often as possible, until you get a favorable response.

As Napoleon said, 'whatever you ardently and constantly desire, you always obtain.' He knew what he was talking about.

HOW TO SET UP A 'DIALOGUE' WITH YOUR SUBCONSCIOUS

Dialogue necessarily implies two parties. In self-hypnosis, those two parties are your conscious mind and your subconscious mind. The word 'dialogue' is not inappropriate to describe the kind of relation that you can establish with your subconscious. It has already been explained how you can communicate with it; to that can be added that you can formulate demands which are extremely specific. In fact, you have probably already done so, without knowing it; and you got a response. Dr Joseph Murphy, an eminent specialist in the field of positive thinking whose books have sold millions of copies around the world, provides a gripping example in his bestseller The Power of Your Subconscious (Prentice Hall).

Here's what Dr Murphy says:

A young man taking one of my courses had the following experience. His father had died, apparently without leaving a will. However, the man's sister assured him that their father had told her he had drawn up a will which would be fair to everyone in the family. All efforts to locate the will proved futile.

Before going to sleep, the young man spoke to his deeper mind as follows: 'I am leaving it up to my subconscious. It knows exactly where the will is to be found, and will reveal the location to me.' He then concluded his demand with the single word 'Answer' which he repeated over and over again, like a chant, before falling asleep. The next morning the young man felt irresistibly drawn to a certain bank in Los Angeles, where a safety deposit box belonging to his father, and which contained the will, was found.

This example may remind you of a similar incident in your own life. Say you lost some precious object like a watch or a ring. You know it's somewhere in the house, but where? All your efforts to find it so far have been in vain. You've gone through all your drawers, and looked in all the places where the object might logically be.

Nothing. You stop and think, trying to remember where you last saw it. Nothing.

You tell yourself, 'I must find this object. I need it. It's valuable.' And then, with all the possibilities exhausted, you give up.

Some time later, in the afternoon or on the following day, while you are thinking about nothing at all, perhaps daydreaming or watching television or chatting with a friend - usually when you are mentally relaxed and your willpower gives way to your imagination - the answer suddenly occurs to you. You intuitively know where to look. You get up and go to the exact place - it's almost a miracle!

Well, there was no miracle. The answer to the problem came from your subconscious. Remember that your subconscious doesn't forget anything; it records absolutely everything. As you distractedly left your ring or watch in an unusual place, your subconscious, always vigilant, was aware of the fact and recorded it.

And later, when you more or less consciously demanded this information by giving your subconscious an order to respond (this authoritarian approach often produces amazing results -you don't ask your brain to do something, you command it, imperatively and categorically), it obeyed and submitted to your demand.

THE IMMENSE WISDOM LYING DORMANT WITHIN YOU

In fact, your subconscious contains an enormous store of wisdom, like a data bank with millions of bits of information.

You subconscious knows exactly what is good for you, and what can help you in your life.

The only thing you have to do is command it. And even more marvelous is the fact that if you know how to communicate with your subconscious, it will never deceive you. All you have to do is make it submit to your commands so that it becomes your ally. You can ask it to do almost anything. It will always respond.

How does it do this? I must humbly admit that this question has not yet been satisfactorily answered: it is without a doubt the greatest mystery still to be unraveled concerning the human mind. But the important thing is that it does work, even if we don't know exactly how. All the rest is secondary. What you should always remember is that:

Your subconscious knows the answer to all your problems

Rest assured, its wisdom is infinite. I have used it myself, hundreds of times, and always with success. Here are a few concrete situations where you can turn to your subconscious for guidance.

HOW TO MAKE A DIFFICULT DECISION

Say you don't know whether or not to accept a job offer. You've been thinking about it for a long time. You've followed the rules, writing down all the pros and cons you can think of. But you still can't find a clear-cut answer. This often happens, and in no way means that you lack decisiveness. In fact most great decision-makers - captains of industry, politicians, military advisers and so on - generally end up relying on their intuition to make a final decision. And what is intuition if not a message sent to you by your subconscious? It analyses all the information you give it with prodigious speed. In addition, it can access all kinds of information stored in its amazing memory - information which you no longer consciously remember, and which can be a determining factor in its analysis of the situation. And that is precisely the information which you may be lacking, and which is preventing you from making a decision.

So you don't know which way to jump. At night, before going to bed (I'll explain exactly how to go about this is Chapter 2) you ask your subconscious for a solution to your problem. Very often you will wake up with an answer, or it might come to you suddenly during the following day. In fact, you will literally have 'slept on it' and come up with the solution.

It may come to you in any number of ways - often mysteriously, and almost always unpredictably. You might run into an old friend whom you haven't seen for years. You chat for a few minutes, and mention your intention to leave your present job at some stage for a position with another company. The friend then says that he just happened to do the books for the company you're thinking of joining and that, confidentially speaking, and only because you're an old friend, he must tell you that their finances are far from healthy. 'At our last meeting, we even discussed the possibility of bankruptcy.'

You break out in a cold sweat. You were so close to accepting the new job, but it could have ruined your career. You had no idea the company was in such bad shape. But in some mysterious way, almost as if you had a sixth sense - and my own experience has confirmed this over and over again - your subconscious guided you to meet this friend, whom you would never have thought of consulting yourself. In fact, you had no idea that he was doing the accounting for the company in question.

The ways your subconscious uses to inform and guide you are mysterious and varied. Sometimes, completely by chance, you'll stumble on an article in a newspaper or book that gives you a precise solution to your problem. An unexpected encounter, like the one just mentioned - almost providential in its timeliness - will often provide you with a solution to your problem. In many instances you will experience a flash of intuition that will determine your course of action. Experience has taught me that it is usually best to listen to your intuition, since it often turns out to be a reliable guide.

This kind of occurrence, of course, does not only apply to professional situations.

However, professional decisions are generally more clear-cut and easier to make than emotional ones, which are often clouded by various degrees of doubt since emotions are, by nature, more fleeting and often difficult to comprehend. You meet someone new whom you like. You're both free. After a while, you start talking about whether you should live together or not. It's a very difficult decision to make.

Ask your subconscious for the answer. It will guide you once again. It knows what course of action will lead you to real happiness and fulfillment.

In fact, you can interrogate your subconscious on all levels: health, business, personal relationships, spiritual matters and so on. Start today. Set up a dialogue with your subconscious, and you will get in touch with the center of your being.

You will have permanent access to the amazing wisdom that has been lying dormant inside you for too long.

HOW TO QUESTION YOUR SUBCONSCIOUS

The technique of questioning the subconscious follows the same rules as that of making suggestions. The question can be a request or a command. Here are some examples:

- 'I find the used car I'm looking for, at a great price. It's in

perfect condition, and meets my needs exactly. My subconscious will guide me to the car.'
- 'I meet my ideal emotional partner, who loves me, and whom I deeply love.'
- 'I find the business partner I need to help me with my work. Our association profits us both.'
- 'I find the house of my dreams - it's exactly what I need. My subconscious will guide me to the house I am seeking.'
- 'I find the money I need to finance my project or to pay my debts.' .-

Of course, the possibilities are as endless as the list of possible needs. As you can see, when formulating commands it is better to be positive and affirmative than interrogative. Instead of saying, 'How can I find the money I need?' it's better to affirm you are going to find it (see p. 29). Even if you don't use exactly this type of formulation, your demand can still bear fruit. For example, you could say something like, 'I absolutely must find the solution to this problem...' or 'I absolutely need to know.' Often, the most important determining factor in your demands, and the ones that will incite your subconscious to find a solution, is your sincerity and the intensity of your desire.

YOUR SUBCONSCIOUS IS ESPECIALLY SENSITIVE TO THE LANGUAGE OF EMOTION

Remember Napoleon's maxim: if you really want a solution to your problem, if you want something sincerely and with all your heart - meeting someone, getting a job, and so on - your wish will generally be fulfilled. But you have to want whatever it is with all your heart, because the demand that you express will be much more powerful if it is supported by corresponding emotions and feelings.

The speed with which your wish is granted is directly proportional to the power and intensity of your desire and feelings. Keep in mind that the subconscious is the seat of emotion. So when you use the language of emotion, you're using a language that your subconscious can easily understand.

You've probably already realized that what motivates people most strongly in all areas of life is emotion and instinct, rather than reason. When we say that a person has a lot of guts, we mean that he or she has a lot of courage. And the word courage has the same root as the Latin word for heart; so being courageous means having a lot of heart. Therefore, don't hesitate to support your demands by desiring whatever it is you want from the bottom of your heart.

A POWERFUL WEAPON FOR GOOD OR EVIL

A word of caution: be careful about what you demand. Not that you have to limit yourself in any way- your demands may refer to almost any facet of life, with no distinctions. It's just that the technique I am offering here, which you will master in a short time even if you only practice for a few minutes each day, is extremely powerful. In fact, it may be the most powerful mental technique anywhere in the world. It is a formidable weapon, and like any weapon it can be used for good or bad ends. As the medieval French writer Rabelais said: 'Science without conscience is the ruination of the soul.'

When you use this technique, make sure that your aims are always beneficial.

Use it to do good, to spread love and fulfillment. In your formulations, you should never wish someone harm or injury. Say you're dealing with an emotional problem in which a third party is involved. Don't try to cause that person to suffer so that he or she will disappear from the scene. That would place you in opposition to the universal laws.

The worst thing that could happen is that your wish, even though it is harmful, comes true. Then you would be sure to suffer in turn, since everyone is subject to the law of cause and effect (or the law of return), which applies on moral and emotional levels just as much as it does to the physical world. And it works in a very precise way, almost to the point of being scientific. It's a little like the law of conservation of energy. Nothing is lost, nothing is created: every action has an equal and opposite reaction. And remember what was said earlier - every thought is an action, and will therefore provoke a reaction.

There is a kind of justice at work here, and the paths it takes are often unfathomable. If your formulation runs against the grain of universal laws, sooner or later you will suffer the consequences. Justice has an infallible memory and a very long arm. Perhaps in a year, or in five or even ten years' time, you will turn a corner and suddenly justice will strike back.

In fact, when you see things from a greater perspective than that of the immediate present, you realize that by doing - or simply by wishing - harm to someone, you are actually hurting yourself. If your desire is based on evil intentions, and if it is realized, you will be the first to suffer: maybe not right away, but one day in the not-too-distant future.

Don't forget that the ultimate law governing our subconscious is one that upholds the principles of life, love and harmony with others. I'll be saying more about this idea in Chapter 3, which contains an infallible method for getting the people around you to love and admire you, and for exerting a positive personal influence on those people by developing a highly magnetic personality.

I have made this rather lengthy digression because I feel it is extremely important for you to understand what kinds of formulations and desires you should be working on. If your aim is happiness- and the quest for happiness is the essential purpose of mankind - love and the fulfillment of a life rich in all ways, then you should only allow yourself to make formulations which lead to the attainment of these aims.

The law of attraction will start working for you, bringing you into contact with situations and people of the same frame of mind, who will help you attain fulfillment. Positive attracts positive, and similarly negative attracts negative; this is infallibly the case. If you allow yourself to cultivate thoughts of hate or envy, or if you integrate thoughts of jealousy, poverty, discord, vengeance and so on into your formulations, you will be sure to attract people and situations of the same kind.

You may object to these warnings, saying that in theory it sounds very easy to entertain only beautiful, noble and generous thoughts, but that in the real world things are not that simple. I agree. Everyone has highs and lows, everyone gets impatient from time to time, or feels envious or even full of hate. But have you noticed that, when you do experience these kinds of negative thoughts and feelings, you always feel awful yourself - you're unhappy, dissatisfied, tense. You may reply that it is precisely because you feel that way that you have negative thoughts. Well, that's true, but allowing yourself to entertain negative thoughts will only make you feel worse.

Thinking negative thoughts is inevitable, especially before you start practicing this method. But it will dissolve all the negative limitations of your personality, allowing you to partake fully of the harmonious flow of life as it should be lived.

HOW TO REACT WHEN YOU HAVE NEGATIVE THOUGHTS OR FEELINGS

There is a way to deal with such negative thoughts and feelings immediately - and I must emphasize that it is of critical importance to react immediately- and that is by applying the law of substitution on p. 27. For example, if you have a hateful thought about someone, even someone who has hurt you and against whom you have a legitimate grievance, replace it immediately with a thought of love and harmony. This may seem simplistic and a little naive, or perhaps you think it sounds like some kind of religious dogma. In fact, it has nothing at all to do with religion, but simply follows the laws which govern the workings of the mind-laws to which we are all subject, whether we know it or not.

Since you are now aware of these laws, you might as well get them to work in your favor. If you do, you will soon reap the benefits. Your life will be richer in all ways. You'll know where you're headed, how to get there, and why you are heading in that particular direction. Your understanding of the events and people around you will be more lucid, and as a result you will experience fewer unpleasant surprises. You will also avoid causing useless suffering, both to yourself and to others.

Words, which we commonly use to express our thoughts, have enormous power.

I hope you are convinced of that by now. Just think of what is possibly the greatest book ever written- the Bible - which begins with the sentence, 'In the beginning was the Word.' Need I say more?

EXCEEDING YOUR LIMITATIONS

The power of words, when used correctly, is truly miraculous. However, I must make one qualification: certain things take longer to come to fruition than others.

Generally speaking, the greater the desire, the more time and energy it takes. So, if you want to program yourself to become the political head of your country, which is not in itself an impossibility, you have to accept that it won't happen overnight.

In the same way, if you want to become a millionaire (and why not? There are already many people who have become millionaires before you, and in fact others are becoming millionaires right now, even as you read these lines!) you have to count on it taking a little time. Maybe not as long as you think, however. This said,

I don't want you to get the idea that you have to limit your desires in any way, that you have to stop dreaming about how you'd like to live. Because don't forget, the greatest limitation a person can have is that imposed by his or her own mind. Faith can move mountains.

The greatest limitation a person can have is that imposed by his or her own mind

Enthusiasm and perseverance can overcome all obstacles. If you really believe you can accomplish something, you will be able to accomplish it. You must not stop dreaming. In fact you must dream, but in a scientific way, by applying the method I am revealing to you here. There's nothing sadder than a person who has stopped dreaming. When one of your dreams dies, a part of you dies too.

Dreaming - allowing yourself a vision of greatness - is truly magical

So don't limit yourself. Just remember that ambitious projects take more time.

And don't underestimate the positive benefits of small victories, either. On the contrary, as I said before, each small victory gives you more confidence, which in turns gives you more enthusiasm and energy. This has a tangible effect on the people around you, and with their help you can move on to greater challenges and more impressive victories.

THE POWER OF IMAGES

A picture is worth a thousand words, as the saying goes. And this is especially true when trying to program your subconscious. We were just talking about the magic of vision, and visualization, in fact, acts as a powerful catalyst for your verbal formulations. We'll now see exactly how that works.

Many people find it easier to use the power of images, rather than that of words, to influence and impregnate their subconscious. That's normal, since we are living in a visual age inundated with movies and TV. And we must remember that the first things our subconscious recorded when we were infants, and before we learned to talk, were images - a host of images of all kinds. I compared self- hypnosis to advertising, when explaining how to use words. The comparison can be extended to help us make use of images as well.

Obviously, advertising 'talks' to you. It repeats the same message (sometimes ad nauseam) or, to be more precise, the same suggestion. But advertising also makes use of images, perhaps even more than words - seductive images, sensual, erotic images, and dream images. In fact, advertising uses all kinds of completely artificial associations in order to motivate us to buy a given product.

You are shown a handsome, sensual young couple on a beach drenched in morning sunshine, sipping their first coffee of the day. You are immediately seduced by the image. In fact, you've needed to get away on holiday for some time now. And the couple are so attractive, so charming.

She has a certain way of placing her lips in the rim of her cup .... And the way she winks at her companion says a lot about the kind of night they must have spent together. He's tanned and athletic. He wears a magnificent watch, which implies a luxurious and wealthy lifestyle as well as good taste. He contemplates his beautiful companion with a look that is both virile and romantic (we're trying to please as many people as possible here!). A gentle breeze rustles through their hair as we hear the sound of waves, backed by some judiciously chosen music.

The spectator is fascinated. Reason is suspended, replaced by the suggestive power of the images. No words are needed. And in fact, the spectator is literally being hypnotized. Advertising tries to reach the subconscious directly by removing mental barriers and defense mechanisms. As you can see, it closely resembles hypnosis.

So the images succeed in putting you in a passive, receptive state. And now comes the pitch. What is the ad trying to sell? Expensive watches? A vacation at

Club Med? No, the product is coffee, a new blend of decaffeinated coffee, with a rich, savory taste that does not affect your health . .. that allows you to remain perfectly relaxed all day long... as if you were on holiday by the sea. And the next time you go to the supermarket, you'll probably recall the image and feel an irresistible urge to try the coffee yourself, even though you've never even thought about using decaffeinated before. Rationally speaking, you know very well that you won't suddenly find yourself on the beach with an enchanting companion as soon as you take your first sip. But your subconscious, which the ad succeeded in reaching, does not know that. It will defy logic, and will infallibly associate that brand of coffee with the beach and romance.

THE AMAZING POWER OF YOUR IMAGINATION

This is usually the way in which advertisers take advantage of the fascinating power of images, often at the consumer's expense. We're going to learn to do the same thing. We're going to learn how to do some 'scientific dreaming', to use the expression I coined earlier. You'll be amazed to discover just how much images can change your life; images and, more importantly, the faculty which generates them - your imagination.

But perhaps you don't trust your imagination. Maybe you think it is only the 'crazy side of logic', as one philosopher put it. I agree that our imagination often causes problems. I would even go so far as to say that imagination can kill a person - it can destroy a life. That's because imagination is the most direct and immediate expression of the subconscious. It is the mirror image of the subconscious, so to speak, and the subconscious is its principal source. This is why people with fertile imaginations -great painters, writers, musicians and so on - are all able to tap into the immense treasure which lies dormant in every person's subconscious. What is inspiration, if not a sudden and involuntary access (later I'll be talking about how you can literally become inspired on command, which has been the great secret of highly creative people) to the storehouse of ideas which is the subconscious?

Of course imagination, when it is badly directed, can be harmful. Napoleon said that 'imagination governs the world'. Personally, I consider imagination to be the supreme human faculty. Unfortunately, too often we underestimate its fantastic power, or we use it for the wrong reasons. This is surely the result of the kind of education we receive. We are taught that dreaming is a waste of time, that the only way to succeed is to rationalize everything, to weigh all the pros and cons with our logic before undertaking anything.

And yet, all of history's great personalities- politicians, artists, inventors, business tycoons or whatever - were, first and foremost, great dreamers and possessed fantastic imaginations. They imagined the future, or their destiny, or their life's work. They saw the path before them clearly, almost as if it were there already, as if they had already achieved what they set out to do -and this despite difficulties and exterior obstacles which, if the people in question had allowed themselves to become distracted, would probably have drained all their enthusiasm and convinced them not to undertake anything in the first place. Such people are often called dreamers, visionaries, idealists and even fools- all of which means that they are imaginative. They know how to exploit the amazing powers of this faculty, which is accessible to anyone, in an exceptionally productive way.

Without further ado, let's take a look at a simple technique which will enable you to make use of the fantastic power of your imagination.

THE SECRET OF IMAGES

Images, like words, can be used in two ways, either to get rid of a bad habit or phobia (for example, smoking, claustrophobia and alcoholism) or to achieve something (buy the house of your dreams, find a better job, start a business and so on). Some people are more visually oriented, while others are more verbally orientated. But in both cases it's a good idea to make use of images, which constitute a powerful reinforcement for verbal formulations.

The basic principle of using images is to act as if the desire you have in mind is already attained. As I have said, the subconscious does not make temporal distinctions. As often happens in dreams, the subconscious perceives everything as if it were taking place in an eternally present moment. So when you imagine something, the subconscious does not distinguish between the image of a desire which will be realized in the future and one that has already been realized.

Therefore, when you impregnate your subconscious with an image of success, you get carried away - or at least your subconscious allows itself to get carried away - by the positive emotions which accompany success, and this reinforces your programming. It's like practicing for success before the fact. Your imagination (your subconscious) is activated, and its forces are set in motion.

An Image - Like a Word - is a Seed...

The technique of using images is subject to the same laws, including the law of growth, as the technique of using words. If you plant images of success, health, happiness, wealth, inner calm and so on in your mind, you will see these images materialize in various life situations with a consistency that is almost mathematical, even if the mechanism whereby these images become concrete remains, for the most part, mysterious. This mechanism is therefore generally referred to- erroneously-as luck or coincidence. The same is also true for negative images-when planted in your mind, they lead to negative life situations.

YOUR IMAGINATION: A PERSONAL TREASURE CHEST

How do you go about using your imagination? In Chapter 2, you'll learn how to induce a state of self-hypnosis. And one of the methods for entering this state uses mental imagery. Once the self-hypnotic state has been induced, all you have to do is imagine the situation you wish to create, in as much detail as possible. What does an orator do when he or she wants to describe something and captivate an audience? He concentrates on details - making sure, however, to choose the most striking and colorful details he can find. Therefore to influence your subconscious effectively, which here plays the role of passive listener while you are the orator (or the cameraman if you like), don't skimp on details. They will help you believe that what you want has already been attained. This technique is called 'mental cinema' and is used in a variety of situations.

To what extent do you have to visualize a positive situation? Some people worry that they are not able actually to 'see' what they imagine (and in fact, I am that way too). But it's not important. The technique is just as effective whether you 'see' your images or not. I imagine things, but in a way that I would call abstract, while other people do actually see the images which excite their active imaginations, as if they had their eyes open during a dream. And yet, despite the fact that my imagination is not as 'concrete' as other people's, I can assure you that I have obtained excellent results by using it to my advantage, and in a scientific way.

Actually, almost everyone uses the technique of mental cinema (which some experts call 'creative visualization', another apt term since that is exactly what takes place) almost all the time. Everyone dreams. And I'm talking about waking dreams, or daydreams. What is a daydream if not a suggestion of images?

Everyone thinks about the future - in fact, it is man's inherent nature to dream.

So many success stores have started in exactly this way: people can already see themselves having attained what they desire. And this applies to almost all aspects of life. You see a beautiful woman in the street, and imagine her in your arms. You see an expensive sports car on a country road, and you can't help but imagine what it would be like to be behind the wheel ....

Obviously, examples of this type of behavior abound. Everyone dreams. The only problem, and the reason most o- these dreams remain unfulfilled, is that they are not methodical, they are not systematic. But now you can learn to dream in the right way - effectively.

THE POWER OF THE LAW OF ATTRACTION

Here are a few examples that will help you understand how to benefit from your imagination.

Say you're looking for a house. You've already spent long hours researching the market, visiting tens or even hundreds of properties. You have an agent working for you. You've told all your friends, and they're keeping their eyes open. But still you haven't been able to find anything suitable. Either it's too expensive, or too far from your office, or it doesn't meet your space requirements, or it needs too many repairs …. You're discouraged, almost ready to give up. And you're under some time pressure as well, since the lease on your flat is up in a few weeks.

This is precisely the time to start doing some mental cinema. Of course, I can't promise immediate success. I can only tell you that I have witnessed hundreds of cases where the technique has worked. And I am tempted to add… 'almost by magic'. I have resorted to mental cinema myself on a number of occasions. Despite the numerous successes it has brought me, I am still astonished every time it happens. The process is so mysterious ….

But let's get back to our problem of finding a house. Is it really impossible to find a house to your liking? No, of course not. And for a very simple reason: whether on an emotional, professional or material level, as is the case here, tell yourself that your thoughts can always produce or create the right conditions for finding what you want. The house you're looking for does exist. All you have to do is use your subconscious, and the law of attraction, to attract it to you. That's exactly what happened to a friend of mine, who later told me about her marvelous adventure. It was the first time she had tried the technique, which I'd explained to her some time before, and at first she was still skeptical. But then she couldn't believe her own eyes. Here's what she told me ....

Once she had put herself into a state of self-hypnosis (see Chapter 2) she tried to see herself, in as much detail as possible, actually arriving at her dream house. This couldn't have been too difficult for her to do, because she'd already spent hours talking about what kind of house she wanted, and even made drawings and plans, thinking that she might build instead of buying one. So she knew exactly what she wanted- a house that looked like the one she'd drawn on paper.

She imagined herself arriving at this house. She admired the front window (large picture window), the front door (heavy oak, classic design). She was impatient to go inside, and her pleasure grew as she entered. She imagined the skylight she'd always wanted (at least the one her husband had always wanted; but no matter, they share everything - even their taste in houses). The kitchen was spacious and functioned perfectly. A fireplace in the living room. Window boxes already in place, which was fine since neither she nor her husband cared much for carpentry.

If you're going to build a dream, you might as well build it to very precise specifications! So in her imagination, the boxes were already filled with a range of healthy, flourishing plants. Outside, behind the house, she imagined a small, well- kept garden where she grew vegetables and herbs.

The only problem was that she and her husband only had a modest amount of capital. In the real world, their dream house would probably cost at least a third more than they were able to invest. However, I had told her beforehand not to worry about those kinds of details during her sessions, but just to let her subconscious absorb the commands contained in the dream.

A week later I got a telephone call. She had just found her dream house. A friend of her husband's, whom she had not seen for years and who lived in another city, had dropped by unexpectedly. He was only in town overnight to do some shopping and take care of some business, and so had decided to visit his old friend. After a pleasant dinner, and despite their insistence that he spend the night, they drove him back to where he had arranged to stay - to a house in a charming suburb (a suburb, incidentally, that they had overlooked in their quest, since they were sure it would be too expensive). My friend was stunned - there she was, standing in front of her dream house, exactly as she had imagined it. And lo and behold, there was a For Sale sign on the lawn!

Except that, despite her dream, the house was surely much too expensive for them. Nevertheless, she asked their guest whether it was true that his friend's house was for sale.

- 'Oh, yes,' he replied, 'Why? Are you looking for a house?' 'Yes, yes we are .... '
- 'Would you like to see it?'
- 'Oh, yes. But it's much too late .... '
- 'Not at all. These people go to bed late. Come on in.'

They let him talk them into it. The owners were playing bridge. Introductions were made. The two couples got to talking, and took an immediate liking to each other. My friend learnt that the house had been up for sale for two months. She said she was interested, and asked the price, the owners said they were willing to let it go for a much lower price than that they'd originally asked. They hadn't found any buyers so far, and in fact no one had even made an offer. They only had a week left before they had to move, since the man had been transferred to a job elsewhere. His company was being very generous with a moving allowance, which would compensate for the loss he would take from making a quick sale. The price he quoted wasn't far off what my friend and her husband were ready to pay. They made an offer on the spot, and it was accepted - all in the space of half an hour!

CREATE YOUR LUCK

All this might sound like a miracle, and yet the story is not fiction but fact. I'm sure you've experienced some happy twists of fate in your own life. And you say: 'Wow! a gift from above!' Most of the time, however, it is a gift from your own subconscious, which you have programmed, probably without being aware of it.

Now you don't have to wait for heaven to send you gifts. You can create your own luck whenever you want.

The kinds of situations where creative visualization can be effective are practically limitless. You can use it to resolve your money problems, to find a better job, to improve your memory or your personal relationships, or to overcome a phobia. I shall be developing each of these topics later in this book, where you will find detailed descriptions of exactly how to apply the method.

This method has been in use for a very long time, by some very illustrious people. The great eighteenth-century German poet Goethe used to resort to self- hypnosis before going to sleep at night, especially when he felt discouraged. He would imagine a friend walking towards him, his face beaming in a broad smile, saying, 'I congratulate you.' Goethe was practicing mental cinema, 'as if his accomplishments that day merited the congratulations of a friend, even if in reality things weren't going as well as he wished. If the technique proved useful to a man of his stature, then it would surely be a mistake to hesitate to use it ourselves.

A more modern personality has also used visualization to soothe his mind and deal with all the problems encountered during the course of the day. I'm referring to the American hamburger king Ray Kroc. In his fascinating autobiography he explains how he would place himself in a state of self-hypnosis at night before falling asleep, and imagine a blackboard on which were inscribed all the problems which were bothering him. He would then imagine himself slowly erasing the problems, one by one. He assures his readers that this simple technique, which he practiced every day, allowed him to sleep like a log, even after working sixteen- hour days and longer. And when we consider the colossal fortune he was able to amass, we must admit that the technique was a total success.

THE BLACKBOARD TECHNIQUE

This technique is actually a variation of what is specifically referred to as the blackboard technique. It is very simple, and many people who have attended my seminars have used it with great success. It has a much broader application than just resolving problems - it can also be used to improve your life. When you want to obtain something, or make a secret desire come true, imagine this blackboard and then see yourself using a piece of chalk to write down what you want. For example, you can visualize yourself writing things like:

- 'I am more and more calm in all situations.'
- 'I am achieving success more and more easily in everything I undertake.'
- 'I find my work more fulfilling every day.'

The list of examples could go on and on. You already know the rules for drawing up effective formulations. Apply them to your particular needs. Write the same sentence on the blackboard a number of times, trying to visualize it more clearly each time. Repetition is equally important when you're working with images. You have to impregnate and saturate your mind with · positive images.

I'll be providing you with a number of variations on this technique throughout this book. But for the moment, start applying the ones I have already explained.

BE ATTENTIVE TO YOUR MENTAL IMAGES

One last point before we move on to the actual technique of self-hypnosis. Like words, images can work either for you or against you. They can remove all the limitations which are preventing you from reaching your full potential, or they can imprison you and force you to play a restricted role in life, a role which you may appear to want to change, but which really, and unconsciously, you accept. By unconsciously I mean that your subconscious accepts it, and that is what is so unfortunate.

We can understand, therefore, that an executive who keeps saying that he can't see himself in the role of president of the company will probably never achieve that distinction. If he can't see himself as president, why should the board of directors or the shareholders do so? He can't see himself as president... in other words, he can't imagine it. He is creating his own mental limitation. In the same way, a person who can't imagine himself speaking in front of an audience will never be able to do so. Yet he may very well possess the ability to become an excellent speaker. He may have more innate talent than someone else who is more of a 'go-getter' and who is not afraid of confronting the public.

So to conclude this chapter, I would like to remind you to pay special attention to the kinds of thoughts, and especially the images, that arise in your mind. You can even take a few minutes, whenever you have some time to spare, to do a little self-analysis. Examine what kinds of images occur to you daily. You may be surprised to discover what you are thinking! One thing is certain – the experience can only be instructive.

But even if you discover some negative things about the way you think, don't get discouraged. The process will be positive in the long run, because you will have become aware of something extremely important in the profound workings of your mind. And this constitutes a decisive and necessary step towards transforming your personality.

SUMMARY OF CHAPTER 1

- Your life is an accurate mirror of your thoughts. Hypnosis is a natural state of consciousness, which allows you to get in touch with your subconscious. The subconscious is programmed, and blindly executes that program. No program is irreversible. You can change your program through self-hypnosis.
- The subconscious can be programmed with words. It is a powerful amplifier, so that everything you think influences it.
- To defend yourself against negative words, you simply have to think immediately of an opposite and positive suggestion.

1. Make your formulations (suggestions) as positive as possible.
2. Make your formulations progressive (Day by day...)
3. Keep your formulations short.
4. Use simple, clear words.
5. Make only one suggestion per session.

- The golden rule of suggestion is repetition. Your subconscious knows the answer to all your problems. It is especially sensitive to the language of emotion. Your greatest limitations are those you create in your own mind.
- The subconscious is very sensitive to images. You can, therefore, influence it by using your imagination. The basic technique, when using images, is to act 'as if' what you want has already been achieved. This places the power of attraction and luck on your side.
- You can also use the blackboard technique. Visualize yourself writing down what you want on a blackboard.
- Be attentive to your negative mental images, and when one arises, create a counter-image to replace it.

2

HOW TO INDUCE THE STATE OF SELF-HYPNOSIS

RELAXATION

Let's start by briefly reviewing our definition of self-hypnosis. It is 'a method which consists of placing your conscious mind in touch with your subconscious so that it can be influenced in a positive way'.

The best way to facilitate this contact with the subconscious is through relaxation. Why relaxation? For one very simple reason which you will readily understand. Our personality - the sum of our habits, ideas and beliefs - is formed without any conscious effort, without the intervention of willpower. It is done without our being aware of it, usually during childhood, when our critical faculties are, for all intents and purposes, nonexistent, and when we are particularly sensitive and open to suggestion. However, through relaxation we can experience what is termed the 'alpha state', usually after only a few sessions.

The alpha state, as explained earlier, is characterized by a slowing down of brain waves when compared to the normal waking state, or 'beta state'. The two other states of consciousness are the 'theta state', which resembles extreme somnolence (and occasionally results in a state of deep relaxation) and the 'delta state', which we experience during certain stages of sleep.

The important thing about the alpha state is that your consciousness remains passive. You 'turn off' the exterior world (without, I must repeat, placing yourself at the mercy of some kind of outside menace, since our survival instincts remain fully operative). This state of relaxation is characterized by feelings of calm, well being and a progressive numbing of the body. Distant memories, images and thoughts begin arising in your mind, and these are signs that you are in touch with your subconscious.

WHEN IS THE IDEAL TIME FOR A SESSION OF SELF-HYPNOSIS?

The best times of day are early morning and at night. Why? Because these are the times when you are closest to your subconscious and when it is most active. In the morning your conscious mind is not yet fully active, and at night it is a little tired from all the activities it has had to perform during the day. This makes setting up a 'dialogue' with your subconscious much easier.

Of course, although morning and night are the best times for practicing self- hypnosis, they are by no means the only times you can enter into contact with your subconscious. In fact, any time of day (or night) is all right, depending on your availability. And the great thing about self-hypnosis is that the more you practice, the easier it is to attain, so that you can do a session at any time, whenever you have the time and the need.

Let me explain. A certain degree of regularity is advisable when practicing self- hypnotism, as with any other discipline. I recommend at least one session per day; if you have the time, do two.

But one good session is quite enough to produce spectacular, profound and lasting results.

It's best to do your sessions at a set time every day, either just before you go to sleep, or earlier in the evening. You will know that this period of the day is reserved exclusively for you, to enable you to relax and work on yourself (the word 'work' is not quite appropriate, since there is nothing more pleasant than self- hypnosis - it's easy, almost like a game, but a game that can change your life and has already changed the lives of thousands of people).

AN EMERGENCY SESSION

Although it's a good idea to schedule your sessions at the same time every day, don't hesitate to resort to self-hypnosis whenever you feel the need. There are moments which can be called emergencies, and when a short session is required to clear your mind. Say you have an important job interview coming up, or you have to make a speech, or go out on a date with someone you find very attractive- don't hesitate to do an improvised session. Even if you only have five minutes to spare, a session will clear your mind and be of immeasurable help. Self-hypnosis is a wonderful took, so why not make use of it whenever you need to, whenever circumstances call for it?

In addition, and as you will soon discover for yourself, just knowing that you can resort to self-hypnosis will give you immense confidence. You'll know that you can handle any situation, where previously you might have become upset or even paralyzed with fear. It's as if you were always carrying a trump card up your sleeve, an unbeatable advantage that you can use whenever you like.

A FEW MINUTES CAN CHANGE YOUR LIFE

What do you think is the most common objection people make when they hesitate to start practicing self-hypnosis? It's: 'I don't have the time.'

But none of these people have tried self-hypnosis even once –otherwise they wouldn't be able to defend this line of reasoning. In fact, self-hypnosis is the one single activity which saves you most time during the course of a day. Twenty minutes per day will go a long way to increase your productivity. You'll be more creative, more efficient, more lucid. You'll also need a lot less sleep, since a few minutes of self-hypnosis a day is the equivalent of about two hours of deep sleep.

In addition, when you do sleep you'll awaken feeling more refreshed and revitalized. Your concentration and memory will improve, as will your ability to make decisions.

Paradoxically (although this seems like a paradox only to those who are unaware of the astonishing benefits of self-hypnosis), it is during those moments in my life when my activities are most demanding, when I have to make a concerted effort and burn the candle at both ends, that I tend to practice self-hypnosis most often. If

I have to write an important sales letter in just a few hours, I don't get all nervous and worried and prepare three or four useless drafts.

Instead, I do a session of self-hypnosis, to clear my mind and summon up all my powers of concentration. Then I command my subconscious to dictate the text I need, rapidly and in a single draft.

If I have the time, I'll let my subconscious do the work overnight (remember that the subconscious is active 24 hours a day, and is always right there at your service if you know how to make use of it). At night, before going to sleep, I provide my subconscious with all the data it needs, having studied the subject matter beforehand. And nine times out of ten, I'll get up the following morning with the ideal letter already formulated in my mind, often with no mistakes whatsoever, as if I had dreamt it. This is normal, since I wrote my perfect letter while asleep. Of course, I do happen to know a lot about writing sales letters already, so it's not as if

I'm doing it for the first time. But my subconscious acts as a precious aid to my thinking process. And one thing is certain - it saves me an enormous amount of time. It can do the same for you. Starting today. Because today, if only you take the trouble to make it happen, is the beginning of a new life for you.

Today is the first day of the rest of my life
Today I start a new life

After a single successful session of self-hypnosis, you will feel so full of energy, so much more confident and concentrated, that you'll never again say you don't have the few minutes you need to devote to it. You'll do the same as me (and thousands of other people) - the more work you have, the tighter your schedule is, the more naturally you will turn to self-hypnosis as an aid for dealing effectively with the situation.

HOW TO PACK TWO DAYS INTO ONE

A few years ago I discovered a way to pack two days into one- to feel just as full of energy at five in the afternoon as at nine in the morning. I'll tell you my secret, and I'm sure you're going to want to try it.

Do you know when I prefer doing my self-hypnosis sessions? It's when I get home from work, before dinner, especially when my evening schedule is very heavy (but also when it isn't and I only have leisure activities planned). You can have a lot of fun when you're full of energy. And my little session of self-hypnosis is like an evening cocktail!

In just a few minutes I can eliminate all the tension and fatigue that have built up over the day. I feel recharged, and ready to face another day. I suggest you try doing the same thing, in order to cut your day in half and benefit from a fresh start when you really need one. This shouldn't prevent you from doing another session later on. The night session is usually best for working on deeper problems like getting rid of negative habits that have been ingrained for a long time, for a more global reprogramming of your life, and when you want to obtain specific responses from your subconscious.

IDEAL CONDITIONS FOR SELF-HYPNOSIS

In principle you can practice self-hypnosis anywhere. But there are two types of sessions. One is the emergency session just described, which can be done at the office, in a waiting room, in a car, at the railway station, at the airport and so on.

Don't worry-no one will notice! And you will automatically wake up if you feel any insecurity, or even if someone approaches to ask you the time. Of course, it is preferable to find an isolated spot, but that isn't always possible. And you still have your regular sessions, which you would usually do in the quiet of your own home.

For these, you should set aside a space and use it all the time- a pleasant, quiet space where you will not be disturbed. Take the phone off the hook if possible, or ask someone to take your calls, or plug in your answering machine. Since it is hard to find a totally silent place unless you live in the country (in any case, absolute silence is not necessary), or if you are likely to be disturbed by ambient noise such as road works or passing cars, don't hesitate to provide yourself with some very soft and soothing background like classical music. There are also CDs and tapes on the market that are designed specifically for relaxation or meditation, and some of these are excellent for self-hypnosis. Choose tapes according to your own taste.

Some people also like to burn a stick of incense or a scented candle to perfume the area. Once again, the choice is yours.

A last detail, but an important one: it is not advisable to practice self-hypnosis after a heavy meal. There is nothing dangerous about doing so; it's just that it will be much harder to obtain satisfactory results. There is one exception to this rule, and that is when you feel the need for an emergency session. Since there's no way to plan for them in advance, you can do a session even after a copious meal. But in general do your sessions at least two hours after eating, unless you've only had a very light meal.

TO RELAX- BREATHE!

As I said earlier, each session of self-hypnosis is preceded by one of relaxation.

With practice, the relaxation stage can be shortened considerably (although you may not want to do so, since it feels great - often resulting in a state that borders on euphoria).

But in order to make sure you relax fully, I recommend using a breathing exercise, which, although simple, is surprisingly effective. I precede each of my sessions with this exercise. It prepares you better than anything else that I know of for the marvelous voyage into the realm of self-hypnosis- a voyage to the very heart of relaxation, serenity and joy, strength and enthusiasm. It a voyage to the center of our selves and root of our being, where we find the secret keys to happiness and success. They've always been there, hidden, and yet within our grasp ....

Why breathing? Because breath is life - animation. The Latin root (anima, meaning both breath and the soul) speaks for itself. Dying means taking your last breath. Living is intimately linked to breathing. And yet, unfortunately, most people do not know how to breathe. They're always short of breath- depressed, tired, apathetic - and nervous.

People who breathe badly are nervous. The reverse is also true - people who are nervous breathe badly. The fact that this pattern works both ways is what's interesting about it. Because this means that the way you breathe has an effect on how nervous you are. And in fact, controlled breathing (like the technique I am going to explain in a moment) has an extremely calming effect on both the physical and mental levels.

Now what do I mean when I say people breathe badly? Two things: they breathe too superficially and they breathe too rapidly. In short, they do not breathe enough.

They breathe incompletely. Complete exhalation is one of the required conditions for good breathing. How can you hope to fill your lungs with fresh oxygen if you don't empty them completely?

So in the little exercise we're about to do, try to exhale as completely as possible before inhaling. And then, as you inhale, use your abdominal muscles. Start by filling your abdomen with air (you may ask how you can fill your abdomen with air if all the air stays in your lungs! Well, the air does stay in your lungs, but when you inhale fully your lungs also expand fully, and push down against your abdomen, creating the illusion that your abdominal cavity is filling up with air).

And don't worry, this won't harm your waistline. On the contrary, internally massaging your abdomen in this way is beneficial for strengthening your stomach muscles and staying - or becoming - slim.

Why abdominal breathing? Because it is more complete and deeper than the two other types of breathing, especially thoracic breathing, where the pectoral muscles do all the work. In addition to being more complete, abdominal breathing relaxes the solar plexus, source of our emotions and much of our tension. You know the expression 'my stomach's tied up in knots ....' and you know the feeling you get when you're scared, when something shocking happens - it's like someone punched you in the stomach. I might add that all actors and actresses, public speakers, singers and so on practice abdominal breathing.

Therefore, after exhaling fully, begin inhaling by letting your abdomen swell out and drawing air down to the bottom of your lungs. As you continue inhaling your chest fills out, perfectly naturally, right up to your throat. That is the way to breathe correctly.

TRY THIS EXERCISE

The following exercise requires a bit of concentration; however, it will in fact improve your concentration and also your memory. It helps to cut off exterior stimulation, too, so that you can concentrate on what is happening inside yourself.

This, in turn, relaxes you and makes it easier for you to enter the state of self- hypnosis. All you have to do is count 20 deep breaths. I can see you smiling already - it sounds almost too simple. How could something so simple accomplish so much? Well, hold fire on your judgment for a moment, and try it.

As you'll see, on your first attempts you'll probably be able to count seven or eight breaths, and then find yourself thinking about other things (as I said, this is an exercise in concentration!). But that doesn't matter. It's completely normal. If the opposite happened (if you were able to concentrate fully for 20 deep breaths), that would be unusual. I have never seen anyone who, on their first attempt, was able to count 20 deep breaths without getting distracted by other thoughts.

Despite these inevitable distractions, you must persevere. Start again at zero.

After a few minutes, and whether or not you've reached twenty breaths, the aim of the exercise will have been achieved. The deep breathing will make you feel calm and totally relaxed, and that is what we're trying to do here- get you relaxed.

Don't do the exercise as if it were some kind of challenge. That will only create more tension. I just want you to become aware of how we in the West are so unaccustomed to concentrating on interior things. Once you find you are breathing deeply and slowly, stop thinking about it. You are now ready to practice a relaxation technique. And in fact, what you have just done constitutes the first step.

Which Position?

Some people prefer sitting (and for emergency sessions this is usually more practical). But for your sessions at home, it's usually best to stretch out on your back. However, if you really prefer the sitting position, go ahead and use it. If you're lying down, do so on a carpet, a sofa or your bed (especially if you schedule your sessions at night, since you can fall asleep afterwards without having to get up and change position).

Clothes

There are no special requirements as far as clothes are concerned, except that whatever you wear should be loose fitting and allow you total freedom of movement. Don't wear belts, ties, girdles, brassieres and so on. At night, a comfortable pair of pajamas is fine.

Length of a Typical Session

I have already spoken a little about how much time you need. However, the minutes you spend in contact with your subconscious are of capital importance, so don't skimp. Above all, try to be as regular as possible. That is the key to success.

At first, if you can manage a session of between 20 minutes and half an hour, that is ideal. With practice, you can reduce the time you need. In emergency cases, when dealing with specific needs, a session which lasts only a few minutes- or even one minute- can provide the results you need since, as you gradually get better at relaxing, you will be able to skip the preliminaries and enter the state of self-hypnosis whenever you want to, in less time than it takes to read this sentence.

Such proficiency usually takes a few weeks of training, it's like developing a conditioned reflex - only this reflex is the most prodigious weapon you could hope to possess.

In all cases, as soon as you start feeling bored, as soon as the exercise becomes monotonous, it is best to stop. You're not there to create more problems for yourself. Sessions should be pleasant and easy. If you're not feeling well, or if you're in a bad mood, don't worry. You can always get back to it another time.

THE IMPORTANCE OF RELAXATION

Scientific studies conducted by world-renowned specialists, notably Hans Seyle, have shown beyond the shadow of a doubt that stress is one of the main causes - if not the main cause - of a host of illnesses, both mental and physical. Stomach ulcers, migraine headaches, cardiac problems and a whole range of disorders called 'psychosomatic' are the result of modern man's inability to defend himself against the onslaught of day-to-day stress.

People who can relax at will are therefore blessed. Their nervous system experiences immediate relief, and their general health improves. Those who are relaxed are better equipped than others to confront the problems of earthly existence. When you are relaxed, your capacity to maintain a positive attitude is greatly improved.

The problem with stress is that it is so common- it has become an accepted part of life, and we often don't realize just how tense we really are. People often need to take a long holiday in order to regain some semblance of a normal, natural rhythm in their lives. However - and this is not an exaggeration - through self-hypnosis, preceded by a session of relaxation, you'll soon feel as if you were permanently on holiday. Life will become a game. You'll regain the enthusiasm, energy and imagination you had in the prime of youth.

The effects of a first relaxation session are almost always the same- completely astonishing. You realize just how stressed you were - that you haven't felt really relaxed for months, or even years. Some people can't even remember the last time they felt relaxed, it was so long ago. Yet at the same time you realize that this is the most natural state there is, and that the state of tension in which you have been living is actually abnormal and terribly destructive. But there's nothing like first- hand experience to convince you that what I'm saying is true.

So without further ado, let's move on to the actual relaxation technique. I'm going to suggest two methods, one or other of which will certainly be right for you. They are both recognized the world over, and practiced with success by millions of people. I recommend trying both of them, and then sticking with the one that works best for you.

To make learning the relaxation method easier I suggest, at least at first, that you stretch out on your back. In this position tensions are naturally reduced and you achieve a state of bodily equilibrium, since every part of the body is supported separately. (In the standing position, for example, all your weight has to be supported by your feet.) When you've become a little more proficient, you can relax in a sitting position if you prefer.

DIFFERENTIAL RELAXATION

To get used to feeling the difference between tension and relaxation, we're going to make use of a certain physiological phenomenon. When a muscle is kept fully contracted for a few seconds it must, immediately afterwards, relax completely in order to recover. This period of automatic recovery can be felt, developed and controlled. And that is what you are going to do.

At first your muscles might feel a little painful. It's a little like starting to practice a sport you haven't done for a long time. This is perfectly normal, so don't worry about it. If you find the exercise too difficult, or if your doctor advises against it for health reasons, try concentrated relaxation (see p. 79) instead.

You can get someone to read you the instructions that follow, or you can tape them yourself and then play the tape whenever you want to do a relaxation session.

Relax . . . feel the extremities of your body vibrating: the top of your head, your toes, your hands .... Turn your hands palms up and make a fist. Squeeze very bard, with all your strength. Tighten your fists and contract all the muscles in your hands and fingers, as hard as you can. Feel the tension and... relax your muscles.

Now start again. Curl your hands into fists and contract your muscles until you feel them vibrating. Go on, tighten your fists, use all your strength, until it starts to hurt... keep squeezing and... relax.

Now concentrate on the muscles in your hands as they recuperate from the effort.

You feel a tingling sensation in the tips of your fingers .... Now you're going to tighten your fists again, and contract the muscles in your forearms, in your upper arms, with all your strength. Go on. Tighten your fists, contract the muscles in your forearms and upper arms... stronger... stronger and... relax completely.

Now start again. Close your fists and tense the muscles in your arms ... tighter ... tighter still ... use all your strength... keep it up... keep going and... relax. Since you've contracted the muscles in your hands and arms so much, you may feel a little pain. Don't worry, just experience how relaxed they feel.

Now let's start the exercise once again· Go on, clench your fists, tighten the muscles in your arms... tighter... tighter ... with all the strength you have ... your arms are trembling... squeeze harder... keep going... keep going and... relax.

Relax your arms completely... Feel the blood circulating in your arms, feel the heat of your blood. Your arms feel heavy... gravity is pulling them down... heavy... heat... concentrate on the feeling in your arms as they recuperate from the contraction... Good.

Now move down to your feet. Point your feet and contract your toes... curl your toes and tense up all their muscles... stronger... much stronger than that... keep it going... keep going and... relax. Feel the vibrations in your feet and toes as you relax.

Now start again. Point your feet, curl your toes and contract your muscles...tighten the muscles in your toes... tighter ... even tighter... tighten them with all your strength... keep it going... keep it going and... relax. Feel the blood circulating, the beat of your blood rushing into your muscles, reviving them.

Now we're going to include your calves and thighs. So we'll be contracting and relaxing your entire legs. Start with your toes... now tense up your calves... your thighs... your legs are as tight as they can be... squeeze harder... harder still and...relax... Good. Just relax all the muscles in your legs, thinking, 'I am relaxed.'

Now start again... feet... calves... thighs... stronger ·.. even stronger... contract your muscles as hard as you can... bold it... just a few seconds more and... relax.

Having contracted your muscles with so much force, you should feel some slight pain in your feet and legs. That's perfectly normal.

Now we're going to start the exercise again. Go on, contract your toes... legs... squeeze bard... very hard... as bard as you can... put all your energy into keeping those muscles tight... squeeze harder... stronger and... relax. Feel bow relaxed your legs and feet are now, bow good it feels to relax and let your muscles recuperate.

Try to become aware of every cell in your legs. Your legs feel heavy... heavier and heavier. Gravity is pulling them down, pinning them to the surface you're lying on.

Now you're going to clench your fists, and contract the muscles in your arms and legs at the same time. Go on... clench your fists, tense up your arms, curl your toes, contract the muscles in your calves ... in your thighs ... stronger... squeeze harder... harder... keep squeezing ... that's it... contract all the muscles as bard as you can and... relax.

Now start again: clench your fists, contract your arm muscles, feet, leg muscles... squeeze harder... harder... use all your strength and squeeze harder... keep it going ...that's right and ...relax.

Now you're going to contract the muscles in your face and neck. Go on, tighten your jaw muscles, your forehead, your neck . . . tense up those muscles... harder... very hard ...use all your strength to keep them tense and... relax.

Now add the muscles in your shoulders and back. First contract your facial muscles and your neck as much as you can. Now tense up your shoulder muscles, and the muscles in your upper back, as if you were supporting a great weight.

Squeeze hard... very hard... come on, you can squeeze harder than that... use all your energy to tense up those muscles... keep it going and... relax. Concentrate on the feeling of relaxation as your muscles recuperate. Feel your blood circulating through all the tiny capillaries in your muscles, revitalizing them with fresh oxygen. Concentrate on your heart beating, pumping blood to all your muscles.

Now you're going to contract all the muscles in your body at the same time, by combining the exercises you've just done. Start by clenching your fists, then contract your arm muscles . . . your feet...your leg muscles... the muscles in your face . . . neck . .. shoulders . . . back ... contract your abdominal muscles . . . your whole body is tensed up . . . squeeze hard...harder...as hard as you can... keep it up... that's right... concentrate and... relax.

Relax completely. You feel your whole body vibrating. Concentrate on your body as your muscles recuperate from the effort. In a couple of minutes you're going to contract all the muscles in your body once again. You're going to do this three times. And when you relax your muscles after the third and last time, you will enter into a state of relaxation that is much deeper and much more interior than you are experienced up to now.

Now you're going to contract all your muscles. You're going to use all your strength. You're going to contract them twice as much as you've done up to now.

All right, go ahead: clench your fists, contract the muscles in your arms...feet ...legs...face...neck...back...your whole body is tight... squeeze harder . . . harder... as hard as you can ...that's right, keep it going... tense those muscles and... relax·

Breathe deeply, and get ready for the second contraction· All right, begin: clench your fists...tighten your arms...feet ...legs...face...neck...back...your whole body is tight... squeeze harder... harder . . . as hard as you can ...that's right, keep it going... a few seconds more and...relax·

Now remember, after this third contraction, releasing the tension will enable you to enter a state of consciousness that is much deeper and more interior than anything you bare experienced before. You will listen only to my voice. All right, go ahead.

Contract all the muscles in your body. Start with your fists ...your arms...feet... legs... face... neck... back ...your whole body is tight... squeeze harder... harder ...as bard as you can... very, very bard... use all your strength... keep it going... that's good... make one final effort to contract all your muscles as bard as you can and ·.. relax.

As you release the tension, you experience a state of consciousness which is very profound, very interior. You feel wonderful ... you are totally relaxed ... you can let yourself go completely, without any tension whatsoever. You are relaxed.

Now get ready to emerge gently from your state of consciousness. Entering deeply into your own body in this way makes you feel very good. You are completely relaxed. Your neck is perfectly relaxed, there's no tension in the nape of your neck at all and, as you'll see in a moment, your sense of vision will be heightened.

In a moment I'm going to ask you to open your eyes. When you do, you will feel wonderful. Your whole body, and especially your bead and neck, will be completely relaxed.

Wiggle your toes. Lightly contract the muscles in your legs. Move your jaw around. Clench your fists slowly and gently. Breathe deeply and stretch· Now open your eyes.

You are perfectly awake, and you can see that your sense of vision if heightened.

You feel reborn, in perfect condition, as if you bad just taken a bath in the fountain of youth. You are charged with energy, in harmony with yourself, with others, with the entire universe.

Now let's look at the second relaxation technique.

CONCENTRATED RELAXATION

Through concentration alone, you will experience that sensation of heaviness caused by the pull of earth's gravity. You will let yourself go, and feel the heat and blood circulating in your body.

Concentrate on your right arm... your right arm is slowly getting heavier . . . it feels heavy... heavier and heavier . . . your right arm is so heavy. Now think: 'My right arm is so heavy. My... right... arm... is... very... heavy. My · .. right... arm... is... is... getting... heavier.. · and heavier . . . it is so heavy . . . it is completely, totally heavy.'

Now do the same thing with your left arm... your left arm is growing heavier little by little... it is getting heavier and heavier. . . your left arm feels so heavy... Think: 'My... left...arm... is... completely... heavy . . . my... left ...arm... is... totally· . .heavy... it feels... so heavy ...so totally... and completely... heavy.'

Now concentrate on your right leg... it is soon going to start feeling heavy . . . your right thigh and calf will get very heavy... heavier and heavier... your entire right leg feels so heavy... your leg is heavy... Think: 'My right leg is heavy... my ... right. . . leg... is... completely... heavy . . . my... right. . . leg... is... getting.. ,heavier ·.. and... heavier... it... is... completely... totally heavy.'

Concentrate on your left leg... relax your left leg... it will soon start feeling heavier . . . your left calf and thigh are getting heavier . . . and heavier. . . .

Your left leg is so heavy... Think: 'My left leg is so heavy ... my... left... leg... is totally... heavy... completely... and totally...heavy.'

Your whole body feels heavy, heavier and heavier . . . it weighs so much... it is a heavy mass... as if there were lead circulating in your veins instead of blood... heavier and heavier... you can abandon your body completely.

Now, as you concentrate on your right arm, you feel a wave of heat rushing through it . .. your right arm is getting warmer... it feels so warm... warmer and warmer... Think: 'My right arm is so very warm... my... right... arm . . . feels . . . so . . . warm ' And your right arm really is warm...completely warm ....

A gentle warmth now pervades your left arm... your left arm is getting warm... your left arm is getting warmer and warmer... Think: 'My... left... arm . . . is . . . completely warm... my... left arm... feels... so very warm .... ' And your left arm really is warm... complete warm and relaxed·

Now the wave of heat moves down into your right leg... you feel the warm blood circulating in your right leg... your right leg is getting warmer... warmer and warmer ...Think: 'My right leg is so completely warm... my... right...leg... feels... warm... it... really... is... warm ... completely and gently... warm ... and relaxed.'

Concentrate on your other leg... you'll feel the heat... it is getting warmer... your left leg is so warm... Think: 'My left leg is completely warm... my left... leg... feels... so... very... warm...it...is... totally...warm... and relaxed.'

Feel the wave of heat as it runs through your entire body. Your heart pulses warm blood through your whole body . . . your whole body feels warm... so very warm... and completely... relaxed.

You feel relaxed... more and more relaxed... the feeling of relaxation spreads... into every muscle of your body... from muscle to muscle . . . and you feel marvelously . . . and completely... relaxed.

PRACTICAL PROCEDURE

All right: now you know how to relax, at least theoretically. In both techniques you proceed step by step, relaxing each part of your body. But how is this done in practical terms? Obviously it isn't enough to read the text in order to become deeply relaxed.

There are a number of ways you can become completely relaxed. You can start by memorizing the text of one or other technique, and then reciting it to yourself mentally, taking care not to leave out any steps. When I say memorize, I don't mean you have to learn the text word for word. Just retain the broader guidelines.

In both techniques you start by relaxing your arms, then your legs, and finally your whole body. It's very simple.

So you can 'memorize' one of the texts. In Chapter 1 I spoke about the amazing power of words. They can be useful when you want to relax. That's why it is very important to repeat mentally the command or suggestion to relax for each step of the exercise. You can use the first person (I) or the second person (you), as the text does. Above all, find out what works best for you. And aim for effectiveness.

For example, repeat the sentence, 'I am relaxing my feet, my feet are becoming more and more relaxed, they feel heavy, so completely heavy, I feel the force of gravity pulling down on my feet...' a number of times, until you actually experience the feeling of heaviness in your feet. You can also add any personal variations which you find effective.

If you don't like memorizing things, or if you think it will be too difficult (it quickly becomes easier with a little practice), you can tape the texts on to a cassette player (adding background music if you like) or have a friend whose voice you find pleasant and soothing tape them for you.

This makes learning the techniques much easier, since the suggestions come from outside. You will be less likely to get distracted, and will passively obey the suggestions being dictated to you. Also, if the reader's voice is calm and melodious it will help you relax. Once you are used to the technique you have chosen you won't need the tape any more and you'll be able to attain a state of deep relaxation almost instantly, whenever you wish.

Finally - and this might be the best option when you are just starting out - you can buy a tape created expressly for this purpose. I have produced two myself, and thousands of people have used them on a day-to-day basis. Others are available from bookshops and other outlets.

A last note: you may very well fall asleep on your first attempts at deep relaxation, even though you don't want to. Don't worry. Although sleep is not the ultimate goal, it's a good sign because it means all your tension has been dissolved.

It is your accumulated fatigue which brings on this sudden sleep, which is perfectly normal and which you should take advantage of, since it is probably deeper and more recuperative than the sleep that you usually get.

You can get back to the relaxation method as a prelude to self-hypnosis next time. It generally takes a few sessions to get past the fatigue and reach the stage of self-hypnosis.

MODERN SCIENCE MAKES A NEW DISCOVERY ABOUT RELAXATION

I cannot conclude this section without mentioning a marvelous scientific discovery which allows you not only to measure your degree of relaxation, but also to improve its quality and depth considerably. It's called Dermo-Biocontrol, and has produced amazing results on a number of students who participated in my seminars on alpha waves and self-hypnosis. Dermo-Biocontrol is a brand name and its equivalent in this country would be an Electrodermal or Galvanic Skin Response (GSR) machine. It is not costly, especially when you consider the extraordinary benefits it can bring to your day-to-day life. And it doesn't only evaluate and develop your relaxation. You can also use it to measure, in a scientific and objective way, your states of mind or those of another person whom you wish to analyze and/or help.

Dermo-Biocontrol is based on the principle of 'psycho-galvanometry' (the polygraph machine, used in lie-detector tests, is based on the same principle). The Dermo, as we call it, is an authentic biofeedback machine, which means that it allows you to detect biological modifications, which are usually unconscious, and convert them into audible signals (in this case a sound which varies in pitch, depending on the intensity of your biological reaction).

Becoming conscious of your biological changes as they occur is the first step on the road to inner awareness and self-mastery. The Dermo makes you conscious of even the most subtle emotional reactions. Then, if you want to, you can learn to control them. There are numerous potential applications in areas like personal development, psychotherapy, psychological diagnosis and psycho-motor re- education. I recommend you to try it for yourself. It made an enormous difference in my life when I first started using it, and helped me become a master in the art of physical and mental relaxation. I know it can do the same for you.

THE METHOD: YOUR PASSPORT TO TOTAL HAPPINESS!

During my years of practical experience and research in the field of self-hypnosis I have been exposed to innumerable methods. I made a serious attempt to make each of them work, and stuck with the one which provided the most rapid and spectacular results, not only for me but also for those who attended my seminars.

As you will see, this method is extremely simple. It is practiced the world over. It has been adopted by thousands of doctors, hypnotherapists and adepts of hypnotism. It is called ocular interruption, and has the advantage of allowing you not only to enter the state of self-hypnosis but also to know for certain whether or not you have really attained that state. (In most cases, especially when they begin practicing the technique, people tend not to be completely sure.)

Once you have relaxed every part of your body, bring your attention back to your eyes, or more precisely to your eyelids. Concentrate on your eyelids. Repeat the following (once again, you don't have to repeat the text word for word - the important thing is to grasp the general idea and the various stages):

Now my eyelids are getting heavy, heavier and heavier. They are getting so heavy that soon I won't be able to open them at all. I will soon enter the state of self-hypnosis. I will feel perfectly comfortable in this state. My eyelids are now very heavy, so very heavy .... I am now going to start slowly counting to ten.

Slowly. Very slowly. And on the count of ten, my eyelids will be so heavy that I won't be able to open them. I will enter the state of self-hypnosis. Soon I won't be able to open my eyelids. When I reach the count often, my eyelids will be so heavy I won't be able to open them. Now I am starting to count, very slowly: One... two... three ...four... five... six . .. seven ... eight... nine... ten .... Now my heavy that I am incapable of opening them .... eyelids are so

Now try to open your eyes. If you can't congratulations! You have attained the state of self-hypnosis. If this is your first attempt, then you are an exceptional candidate· As we say in professional jargon, your level of auto-suggestion is probably very high.

But if you didn't succeed, don't worry. It's actually completely normal not to attain the state for the first few times. Don't consider it a failure in any shape or form. My experience has taught me that even very gifted subjects usually need five or six sessions before the ocular interruption technique works and they enter the state of self-hypnosis. In my own case, despite my firm convictions and previous experience in alpha relaxation, eight sessions were necessary.

Was I less gifted than others? I don't think so. Especially if I judge myself by the extraordinary results I obtained shortly afterwards. There's one thing you shouldn't forget: my experience with numerous students has proved to me that a slow beginning in no way means that you will not achieve spectacular results in the end.

Eight sessions may seem like a lot. But if you consider that I did one session a day, it only took a week and a day to succeed .... A week and a day is a very short period of time when you're talking about literally transforming your life. I must admit that, looking back and knowing what I accomplished through self-hypnosis,

I would have been ready to wait months instead of just a few days. But rest assured, you won't have to wait that long. Just remember that 99 per cent of people who try do succeed in attaining the state of self-hypnosis.

All right, back to our method. If the ocular interruption technique worked for you, fine. You are now ready to begin working on your subconscious. We'll be looking at just how you go about doing this a little later on.

If you were able to open your eyes despite the suggestions you made to keep them closed, take a few deep breaths and do the ocular interruption exercise again.

Many people succeed on the second attempt. But never make more than two attempts per session.

In the following section, we'll be looking at a few exercises for developing your technique of self-hypnosis. I suggest preceding your second attempt with one of these exercises, especially if your first did not succeed. This will improve your chances for success.

Therefore, to summarize what I've just said, if it doesn't work the first time around - which is usually the case (and in some cases, even when ocular interruption does succeeds there are occasions when you find it more difficult or feel less in the mood) - do one of the training exercises.

Here's how to proceed:

1. First attempt at ocular interruption.
2. Training exercise.
3. Second attempt at ocular interruption.

Whether or not your first try at ocular interruption worked, do the second step (mental programming), which is really the most important. I must emphasize the fact that, even if you do not immediately attain the state of self-hypnosis, you should do the second step anyway. You will get results, often quite spectacular ones. Remember that, because of your breathing and relaxation exercises, you have already attained a certain degree of passivity. Your consciousness is directed inward sufficiently to allow you to access your subconscious effectively.

Mental programming is actually the aim of self-hypnosis- it is the path to success and happiness. You have already stepped through the doorway leading to the treasure house that lies at the center of each human being (and which, unfortunately, most people don't know about). There you will find the power to control your own destiny. You are now in command, no longer governed by others or by circumstance.

At first you are experimenting, discovering what relaxation and self-hypnosis are all about. As you have seen, the method is simple. You may even think it's too simple to be effective. Don't fall into that trap - the simplest things are often the most effective. Would anyone once have believed that splitting an invisible and infinitesimally small object could produce a reaction as powerful as the atomic bomb? Yet today, everyone accepts it as a common fact.

And in fact, self-hypnosis is as powerful as atomic energy when it comes to changing your personality. As soon as you start using it, right from your very first session (and even if it takes some time for you to realize what is going on inside yourself), a chain reaction is unleashed which will soon transform and finally ignite your inner energy, which has been imprisoned for too long.

So in the beginning you are an explorer, gradually discovering a new, and usually very pleasant, state of mind. You will surely wonder why you didn't make this discovery a lot sooner, and I'm sure you'll want to share it with your family and friends. But what are the characteristics of this state of mind you are about to discover?

You will experience a state of profound relaxation, with a marked tendency to remain immobile. This is quite normal. You'll feel so good that you won't want to move. You'll even wish the state could continue indefinitely. All your muscles will feel heavy and free of tension.

Some important advice: after your initial sessions, which will be above all of an exploratory nature, start planning your mental programs in advance. Decide which problem you want to deal with, or which aspect of your personality you want to work on. Write the text you will use. Your sessions should not be improvised. The mental programming part should take at least half the time allotted to each session.

It is the key to success, so make sure to get it right.

HOW TO COME OUT OF THE STATE OF SELF-HYPNOSIS

It's very simple. You actually do the same as you did during the self-hypnotic state - give your subconscious a command by mentally repeating some version of the following words:

Now I am going to emerge from my state of self-hypnosis. When I return to my normal state, I will feel perfectly relaxed and rested. My head, neck and shoulders will be free of tension. On the count of five, my eyes will open and I will begin moving slowly. One... two... three... four...

Wiggle your toes, move your hands, your jaw, flex the muscles in your legs, stretch like a cat... and open your eyes. You see, it's that easy. Sometimes - though very rarely - a subject may experience some difficulty emerging from the state of self-hypnosis. But since self-hypnosis is a completely natural and extremely pleasant state to be in, don't worry if it happens to you. Just count to five once again, after ordering yourself to open your eyes. Or do some more mental programming, and then open your eyes. Or simply abandon yourself to the feeling of well being you experience under self-hypnosis. In any case, people rarely stay hypnotized for longer than half an hour. Either you awaken spontaneously, or you fall asleep.

HOW TO INTENSIFY YOUR SELF-HYPNOSIS SESSIONS

I suggest two simple and effective methods that can be used to help you when you're first starting out, or on occasions when your frame of mind is not disposed to attaining the desired state, or simply to increase the scope and effectiveness of your sessions. The first method is called finger contact.

Your are in your normal position (on your back) and have completed the first stages of relaxation and self-hypnosis.

First Exercise: Finger Contact

Concentrate on your right hand (or your left hand if you're left-handed), especially on your thumb and index finger. At this point in the exercise, your fingers should not be touching. In fact, the aim of the exercise will be to bring them into contact. Repeat the following suggestions to yourself, and at the same time try to visualize the movement of your fingers:

My thumb and index fingers are slowly moving together. They are moving so slowly that the movement is almost imperceptible. They get closer, closer, slowly, relaxed, completely relaxed. Slowly your fingers move together, until they are touching, and I enter the state of self-hypnosis. It is a deep state, very deep. A state of incomparable calm. As soon as my fingers touch, my state of self-hypnosis will intensify. I'll feel even more relaxed. Now my thumb and index finger are touching.

And I enter a deeper state of self-hypnosis. As soon as my fingers touch, I go deeper into my self-hypnosis. And they are touching. . . now.

The exercise takes one or two minutes. Do it very, very slowly. Your fingers should come together very gently. Keep concentrating on the movement as you visualize it happening. It is very effective, and very simple to do. Now let's look at the second exercise.

Second Exercise: Arm Levitation

You're in the same position- lying on your back. Concentrate on your right hand (or left hand if you're left-handed). Feel your arm growing heavier. It is very heavy. Your whole arm feels heavy. It almost feels as if your arm is sinking into the mattress or carpet you're lying on. As if it were turning to liquid.

Now you feel a wave of heat flowing through your hand. Visualize your fingers dearly. They are completely relaxed, and very heavy. Now a feeling of lightness replaces the feeling of heaviness in your hand. Your hand is becoming luminous.

Light as air.

Now you are going to start raising your hand slowly. As if it were being pulled up by an invisible string. As if it were moving all by itself. And as you visualize the extremely slow movement of your hand rising into the air, you are going to repeat the following text- not word for word, but the essence of the text, as you would for any formulation. You can add things, or leave things out, according to your preferences.

My band is now getting lighter, much lighter. It glows, surrounded by a gold-colored light. The light enters my bands, and radiates from its center, lighting up my fingers. My skin starts shining. And little by little, my band lifts up, very slowly.

My whole arm now feels very light. It lifts off the ground, luminous, light as a feather. Light as the wind. Slowly my arm rises. The lightness in my band spreads to my forearm, my elbow, my shoulder. My arm is lifted by some mysterious force.

It rises slowly, and then my band starts moving towards my forehead. Very slowly.

I see it descending towards my forehead, released of all tension, of all rigidity. My band, luminous and light, moves imperceptibly slowly towards my forehead. Soon it will touch my forehead. And this contact will seem like magic.

As soon as my band touches my forehead, my self-hypnotic state will reach a depth I bare never known before. I will attain a state of incomparable relaxation.

Deep, very deep relaxation. My band is getting closer to my forehead, moving very slowly. I can feel it, I feel my band's luminous radiation, like a light erasing all my worries, and allowing me to experience a state of deep, deep well being. Now my hand is just a couple of inches from my forehead. I can feel it radiating even more strongly. Now my hand touches my forehead. Light and luminous. It transmits its energy and light to my head, and then to the center of my being. I am now in a state of deep self-hypnosis. Very, very deep....

Let your hand rest on your forehead for a few minutes. Feel the deep wave of relaxation flowing through you. Now bring your hand back to its original position, more rapidly than you did when raising it.

The duration of the exercise varies according to the individual. But in general, it's best to do it as slowly as possible, allowing at least a minute or two. You'll soon see for yourself how easy it is, and the effects are magical.

WHAT TO DO IF IT DOESN'T WORK

First of all, don't get discouraged, it usually takes a few sessions to succeed, as I've already explained. But perseverance and regular practice will always pay off in the end. And don't forget that you can still influence your subconscious even if you don't reach the state of complete self-hypnosis.

Here's some advice that may help you. Read over the instructions I've given you so far. Maybe you've forgotten one of the steps.

One of the obstacles I've often encountered among people is an over-skeptical attitude to self-hypnosis. You have to have an open mind at least. Obviously, if you've taken the trouble to obtain this book, you do have an open mind to some degree. But sometimes, despite a willingness to try the method, people are persuaded beforehand that it won't work. Tell yourself that if you don't believe you can succeed, you are greatly limiting your chances. So be positive. Tell yourself you can succeed - easily. As Chopin used to say to his students, 'If you want to play the piano well, you have to believe you can play.' In the same way, if you want to attain the state of self-hypnosis you have to believe you can do it.

Another piece of advice: during the self-programming stage, repeat the following formulation: 'My aptitude for self-hypnosis is growing from session to session.'

Otherwise an equivalent formulation that works better for you. This will get your subconscious working for you.

If, despite all your attempts, you still fail, you may want to consult a competent hypnotist. Ask him or her to give you a posthypnotic suggestion that will make it easier for you to induce the state of self-hypnosis successfully.

CREATE YOUR OWN METHOD

Self-hypnosis is a solitary art. You are alone with yourself. You work on the most intimate part of your being - your subconscious. It's difficult for an author to come up with a method that corresponds exactly to the tastes and needs of everyone. That's why I have included variations on the various techniques I am teaching you. Try them, combine them to suit your own taste, and adapt them to your own personality. In this way, you can create your own method.

One variation which is very useful and effective is best done in a seated position.

Get comfortably seated, either on a couch or on the floor (using a carpet, thick blanket, straw or similar mat), in the cross-legged position. Stare at the flame of a candle, or at a black spot on a piece of paper, or at the tip of an incense stick (it doesn't really matter what you use - any small object will do, especially if you're not at home and feel the need for an emergency session).

Stare at the point for not more than two minutes, while repeating the following formulation four or five times:

My eyelids are heavy, they are growing heavier and heavier. . . . They are so heavy I will soon have to close them, and when I do I will enter the state of self- hypnosis.

If your eyes close and you cannot open them without instructing your subconscious by using the 'count to five' technique, then you have succeeded.

I am now going to suggest a few more techniques. Actually, there are a host of techniques designed to induce a state of self-hypnosis. If you find any elsewhere, feel free to use them. Finding one that works for you often depends on your personality, your taste and your preferences. Here's one designed for people who like nature, gardens, flowers and so on. It's called the 'classical rose' technique.

The Classical Rose Technique

Imagine a magnificent rose, preferably red. The rose is a universal symbol and has profound connotations in the minds of most people. A rose represents love, beauty and life. Imagine each petal of the rose opening, blossoming. And as each petal opens, one of your muscles relaxes, releasing all its tension and stiffness.

First the muscles in your neck and shoulders, where much of the tension of the day accumulates. Then your arms, which grow heavy as they relax. More petals unfold, and your stomach and intestines release all their tension and relax completely. The rose opens more fully, and the feeling of well being spreads down into your legs, your feet. You are now completely relaxed and serene.

You are a vision of beauty and fulfillment, like the dosed rosebud opening into a radiant flower. You identify with the rose-you are the rose.

Imagine this radiant, sweet-smelling rose in the area of your heart. It vibrates, radiating a warm golden light. It sends waves of light outwards into space, filling the entire universe. The waves rebound off the people you love, and return to you multiplied tenfold in intensity, so that they dazzle you with golden light. Your heart and this radiant rose are one. They form a magnetic center of pure love, light and harmony. Doing this exercise for a few minutes, especially if you are able to visualize the radiant rose blended into your heart, will do so much to open up your emotions and get rid of negative tension. You will gradually feel a great current of love spreading through you, coming from the center of your being and radiating outwards all around you.

Feather Relaxation

This technique is suited to persons with a more childlike personality. As a feather slowly descends towards the ground, swirling gently on the currents of air, you gradually reach a state of deep relaxation. It's best to visualize a white feather - a perfect, dreamlike feather. See it floating gently down out of a perfect clear blue sky, against which the white feather stands out in vivid contrast. It descends slowly, very slowly. At each stage, as the feather gets closer to the ground, you become more relaxed. Your muscles lose all their rigidity, becoming heavy, very heavy, and completely relaxed. And finally, at the precise moment when the feather touches the ground, you enter the state of self-hypnosis.

Wave Relaxation

This is one of my favorite techniques. The seaside is certainly one of the places most conducive to relaxation: people take holidays by the sea to regenerate their minds and bodies.

Imagine the ocean. Imagine a blue wave, deep aquamarine blue, very large and luminous. Although powerful, the wave moves slowly, peacefully. It rolls over you, lifting you gently. The water is an ideal temperature, perfectly warm, and its gentle warmth envelops your entire body. You feel marvelously relaxed. You feel light, as if you were floating. You are floating in the ocean. One wave follows another. The first recedes into the distance, taking with it all the tensions accumulated during the course of your day, all your negativity, all your frustrations. The wave carries all these far away, forever. You are rid of them completely.

Then another wave rolls in, even more immense than the first, a deeper shade of blue and luminous, shimmering as it reflects the light of the sun. The wave first touches your head, then descends along the length of your body, relaxing each muscle, making your body light, luminous and relaxed. This wave too rolls off into the distance, carrying away any remnant of tension or frustration, any nagging problems you may still bare. Now you are totally calm and relaxed.

Another wave appears. This one seems to flow right through you, penetrating and inundating you, so that your body becomes one with the wave, with the warm water of the sea. The warmth is so pleasant, and the luminous water envelops your body. You are nothing more than this wave. This wave of total relaxation, happiness, harmony and peace.

And now, you see another wave, far in the distance, even bigger than those before it. It is majestic, towering, moving slowly, dominating the entire horizon.

And you know that as soon as this wave touches your body, you will enter the state of self-hypnosis. Deep hypnosis. You will become one with the wave. It will carry you away, light, completely relaxed, in total harmony with the universe of witch you are a part. Your body will become luminous, lifted by this immense wave. It's getting closer now, closer and closer. You can already feel a profound sense of calm overcoming you. You can smell the beautiful odor of the wave, a rich, soothing odor of clean ocean air. And now, the wave touches you, lifting you high in to the clear sky, flowing all around you. And you enter the state of self-hypnosis.

The Circle of Light

Now here's a final exercise:

Imagine a sphere of light surrounding your head. The light is golden, like the light of the sun at dusk, and forms a halo around your head, shining through it so that your head itself becomes the halo of light. The light enters your body through all the pores of your skin, bathing every cell of your body, every one of the millions of cells in your brain. The light creates a feeling of tranquility, peace and gentleness right down into the center of your being.

Now visualize your head as clearly as you can. It is luminous, and it will retain some of this luminosity in your day-to-day life. Imagine that, because of this halo of light you are visualizing around your head, you are becoming a radiant being.

Really radiant. Your face shines with a new light. Your personality becomes magnetic and powerful, attracting the people around you by the simple force of your presence. Feel the light completely dissolving all your problems, frustrations and tensions. The light dispels any dark, shady areas of your being. It bathes and illuminates every corner o/your brain, every corner of your head, every facet of your life.

Now imagine the sphere moving down to your chest, and situating itself around your heart. The light dispels all your negative emotions and fills you with a sense of courage and enthusiasm, hope and strength. The light bathes your heart and your lungs. You can already feel yourself breathing better, more deeply and calmly. Your lungs become radiating light. Your heart is nothing more than a center of energy, a sun, nourished by the circle of light and nourishing the light in turn.

Now the sphere of light moves once again, this time down to the area of your stomach and abdomen. You see the light encircling all your organs, your liver, your intestines, your kidneys, your spleen. Your organs are bathed in this re- generating light. They relax completely, and feel full of energy, recharged and ready to fulfill their respective functions.

The light now moves down and surrounds your hips and genitals. It fills your sexual organs with force and vitality. It regenerates them completely. At the same time it dissolves all your sexual frustrations, all the problems you may bare that are connected to sexuality. They are completely dissolved by this radiant light.

Your body feels lighter and lighter.

And the sphere of light moves once again, this time down to your legs. Imagine your knees bathed in the sphere of golden light. Then your feet, where you accumulate so much tension and pressure every day - the light surrounds your feet and dissolves all the tension in them. The circle is closed. You are illuminated from bead to foot, bursting with the light of harmony. Feel yourself becoming this light.

You are radiant, full of feelings of love and peace.

Now imagine a larger sphere of light, more oval, hovering over your body. You see it above you, and you find it fascinating, brilliant. This light is a pure vibration of harmony and love. You see it slowly descending towards you. You are impatient for it to reach you. You know that in just a few seconds it will touch your body, like a soothing balm of light and tranquility. You know it will envelop your entire body, releasing all the pressure inside you, dissolving all your problems. It will bring you a deep and lasting peace. It will illuminate your entire being. Your whole body will feel magnetized. You see the oval of light take the form of your own body as it slowly descends, closer and closer to you.

And you know that when it touches you, you will enter the state of self-hypnosis.

The techniques I have just described are known the world over, and usually have a very powerful effect. Try them all, even if you don't find them appealing at first.

Then, once you've tried them, keep using the one(s) which made you feel most relaxed. You don't always have to use the same technique. Choose the one which is most appropriate to your mood at any given time.

Sometimes you may prefer the wave technique, at other times the circle of light.

It's completely up to you.

Now that you are familiar with the theory and techniques of self-hypnosis, we can begin our discussion of practical applications. There are lots of them, and they relate to all aspects of human activity.

Incidentally, I should remind you that, in order not to overload your subconscious, it's best to work on only one problem at a time. When that problem has been solved, you can move on to another one.

You will notice, however, that success in a specific area will also have a more general effect. A person who uses the method to lose weight, for instance, will also regain his or her self-confidence and feel endowed with a love of life he or she may have lost.

SUMMARY OF CHAPTER 2

- Relaxation is the best way to gain access to the subconscious.
- Morning and night are the best times to practice self-hypnosis.

You can, however, resort to 'emergency sessions' whenever necessary.
- Self-hypnosis will save you a lot of time. Create a quiet, pleasant space in which to do your sessions. Use soothing background music if you like. Take the phone off the hook. Avoid sessions after heavy meals. You can lie down, or sit comfortably. Make sure your clothes are loose and do not constrict your movements, especially your breathing.
- Start by doing 20 cycles of abdominal breathing, then relax your entire body with the differential relaxation technique (tightening various muscle groups, and then relaxing them).
- After a few sessions, you can change to concentrated relaxation. You may want to use a Dermo-Biocontrol apparatus to help you.
- The ocular interruption technique, while counting down from ten to zero, will automatically put you in a state of self-hypnosis. If you have trouble achieving this state, do one of the intensifying exercises such as finger contact or arm levitation, and then use the ocular interruption technique again.
- To come out of self-hypnosis, count from one to five and then start gently moving the various parts of your body.
- You can develop your own personal method, based on one of these variations.
- staring at an object, such as a candle flame or an incense stick
- rose technique
- feather technique
- wave technique
- circle of light technique

③
HOW TO UNBLOCK YOUR REAL PERSONALITY

An individual's personality is a passport to his or her success, from all points of view. What do we usually remember about people? More than their physical beauty, the clothes they wear or their voice, we tend to retain an impression of their personality. The qualities I have just named are all part of someone's personality.

But real personality is an interior quality, or more accurately an aura of energy which emanates from the deepest part of a person's being.

A recent study conducted in the USA shows that 85 per cent of people's success depends on their personality. The remaining 15 per cent corresponds to their skills and experience in their chosen field of endeavor. Many successful people have an implicit understanding of this fact.

Take politicians, for example. Most people vote more for a candidate's personality than for his or her political views. They are voting for an image, often carefully constructed for (and by) the media. Did you know that John F. Kennedy, while still a student and before deciding to enter politics, was a very introverted person, more likely to become a writer or a professor than a public figure? If he had not decided one day to open up and become more extrovert-in other words to transform his personality completely – he would certainly never have become President. He would never have been able to generate the extraordinary popularity he enjoyed.

So 85 per cent of your success depends on your personality. Food for thought, isn't it. This just proves that the best investment for success is in your own personality. 'That's all very well,' you say, 'but how am I supposed to acquire a great personality and succeed in everything I do, without appearing to put on airs or look like a fake in other people's eyes?' Well, the answer is simple. Transforming your personality doesn't happen overnight. You will succeed, but only after a few months of working on yourself. However, a degree of change does occur as soon as you begin. It just takes a bit of time for that change to have a profound and lasting effect. It all depends on where you are when you begin, and especially on the image you have of yourself and the kinds of obstacles blocking the full development of your potential.

You know you have potential. You know you could be more effective, more confident, more loving (and loved), and a generally happier and more positive person. But you don't know how to release all that potential. Don't worry, most people are just like you; they use only a tiny part of their full potential – rarely more than 10 per cent.

What obstacles are preventing you from acquiring the personality you've always dreamed of having? Well, the first obstacle was probably the fact that you were unaware of your own possibilities. But that isn't the case any longer, since you now know that you have access to a formidable reservoir of knowledge and energy – your subconscious mind. What other obstacles, then? Most of them are unconscious, and are the result of our education. Personality, for the most part, is not inherited; it is the product of a process of conditioning. The encouraging thing is that what was programmed into you can also be unprogrammed, and then replaced with a better program. But the real obstacle to developing a positive personality is the image you have of yourself.

Your personality is based on who you believe you are

Nothing more, nothing less.

Your limit is your mental self-image

If you want to break free of your limits, then break free of your mental image.

BECOME A WINNER!

People who have a winning self-image project that image to others, and really do become winners. Haven't you noticed that we usually react to people in accordance with the image they project? If someone appears hesitant and unsure of him/herself, we are not favorably impressed and tend not to find that person credible and reliable. Yet that same person may be extremely gifted and exceptionally intelligent, and an expert in his or her field. The problem is the image he or she is projecting. Think about it, because the image factor is of capital importance - in it lies the key to your transformation.

Now let's do a little self-analysis. What image do you have of yourself? What image do you think you project to others? Are you a winner or a loser?

If you feel you're a winner, that's fine. But self-hypnosis will still be useful to you since it can increase your coefficient of success - it can make you even more magnetic than you already are. If your self-analysis led you to the conclusion that your self-image is that of a loser, don't worry too much about it. You've already taken a giant step forward, just by becoming aware of it. It's like a doctor's diagnosis, which is the first step towards finding a cure.

HOW TO OVERCOME AN INFERIORITY COMPLEX

Psychologists have demonstrated that most people suffer to some degree from an inferiority complex. We underestimate ourselves. And most of the time we are wrong to do so. Sometimes it's because we have experienced failure, or a series of failures, and this shrinks our self-image. Sometimes it's due to what psychologists call 'the Pygmalion effect': You become what your parents, teachers and peers expect you to become. Their expectations have forged your personality, most often in a negative way. For example, you may have overhead someone say something negative about you:

- 'He'll never amount to anything'
- 'He won't get very far in life'
- 'He's so clumsy, he's incapable of doing anything with his hands...'

That's the perfect program, unfortunately, for creating an inferiority complex.

But don't forget one thing: nine times out of ten, a person's belief that he or she is inferior is not based on fact. It's purely imaginary. And now that you know you have the ability to break through your own limitations, you need not put up with this feeling of inferiority any longer. You are going to get rid of it once and for all.

And since you are aware of the power of self-hypnosis, you already have a head start.

DEVELOP YOUR SELF-CONFIDENCE

As you rid yourself of your inferiority complex, you will become much more self-confident. You'll be amazed at your own audacity in certain situations. You'll be surprised at the way you can handle situations that had you paralyzed with fear before. You'll have presence and find it easy to deal with other people, and you'll never be at a loss for words. Confidence is of key importance. If you don't have confidence in yourself, why should other people have confidence in you?

In Chapter 1, I explained that there are two ways to program the subconscious through words and through images. Depending on your temperament, choose one of the two - or, better still use both.

I'm going to recommend a formulation that I've been using myself for years.

Because, surprising as it may sound, I too suffered from a kind of inferiority complex - for years I was extremely shy, and had great difficulty dealing with public situations. I've come a long way since then. No doubt the people who knew me back then wouldn't recognize me now if they saw me leading one of my seminars or chairing one of my conferences.

Of course, I'm not the only person who has had to overcome a fear of speaking out in public, nor is there anything exceptional about my case. Many of my students have confided that their friends and colleagues were amazed by the radical transformation in their personalities. Are we any different from you? Not at all. All we did was apply this method, and you can do the same. I know it will bring you the same measure of success.

Here is the formulation which, as you will see, is simply a variation of the one presented in Chapter 1.

Day by day, in every way, I am becoming stronger and stronger, and more and more confident

This formulation is dynamite. Why does it mention strength? Because inner strength is the source of confidence. We could even set up the following equation: great strength equals great self-confidence. Being strong means feeling in control, not only of yourself, but also of the events taking place in your life. Being strong means that you have taken hold of the reins of your destiny. And that is why this suggestion is so powerful. Your confidence will grow rapidly as you develop your inner strength. Repeat the formulation ad infinitum. Saturate your mind with its meaning. Your confidence will soon become contagious and spread to the people around you. Nothing will be able to stand in your way. You will overcome any and all obstacles. You'll turn your back on failure, never doubting your eventual success. And you will achieve success after success, in everything you do.

CHANGE YOUR IMAGE BANK

Now let's look at the second technique, the one using images. We are going to do some mental cinema. Why? Because your feeling of inferiority, your lack of confidence has created a bank of images in your subconscious, all dealing with failure. You are continually seeing yourself in difficult or unhappy situations, where your ego is made to appear ridiculous. We are going to erase these images once and for all, and replace them with a new set of images - positive images, images of success.

There are two avenues of approach. First, you are going to dig into your store of memories and find the happy moments in your life when you experienced success (even limited success). And you are going to relive

these situations in your mind. It could be your boss congratulating you for some work well done. It could be someone expressing his or her love for you, or complimenting you. You may recall winning a contest or some kind of competition. It may have been during the course of an evening with friends, when you made some hilarious remark or found the perfect repartee (as your confidence grows, you'll soon develop an ability to say the right thing at the right time). It could also be a moment of tenderness or intimacy with someone you love. What matters is that when you relive these moments you feel good, you feel important. And by reliving these moments you can reconstruct your self-confidence, since the subconscious, as we saw in Chapter 1, does not make any temporal distinctions.

In the second avenue of approach you will use the 'as if...'. You are going to visualize yourself in public situations, feeling at ease, smiling, surrounded by people who enjoy your company and appreciate what you have to say. You will imagine these situations in as much detail as possible - the setting, the people, exactly what is said and what goes on. You will visualize a host of such situations.

They may involve a man or woman whom you find attractive, but whom you haven't dared approach as yet. Imagine yourself with that person, enjoying a good meal, walking hand in hand through the park, and so on. Your loved one smiles, letting you know that the feeling of love is reciprocal. And you feel completely confident. You spontaneously come up with the right thing to say, and your partner finds you charming and witty. Your gestures are perfect, you are tender and romantic. You imagine the situation as if you have already been lovers for a long time. The results will amaze you. The power of thought will work its magic, not only on you, but on the people around you as well.

An Example

You can resort to this technique for any situation which requires confident action. Say you have to make a speech in front of a group of people for the first time in your life. Just the thought of it terrifies you. Your throat gets dry, your hands are moist with perspiration. Imagine yourself making the speech, confronting your audience.

Once again, visualize the scene in as much detail as possible. Create an ideal situation, with yourself as the star performer. People start by giving you a warm round of applause as you make your entrance. A joke comes to mind, and through your sense of humor you immediately win over your audience. You have prepared your notes carefully, but you don't really need them and lay them aside. You know your text. Frequent bursts of applause punctuate your delivery. When it's over, you get a standing ovation and people rush up to congratulate you.

You see, it's simple. Of course, I can't provide examples for every possible situation. But you can. Just create a positive scene that meets your requirements.

Imagine the perfect situation, and live it in advance as as it had already happened.

Your confidence level will multiply tenfold, and very often things will work out exactly as you imagined they would. One thing is certain: your increased confidence level will be apparent both to you and to those around you. And this is only the beginning. Each success will consolidate your newfound confidence and make it grow even stronger.

HOW TO CREATE A NEW PERSONALITY

Anyone can do it, on two conditions (and these conditions apply to all applications of self-hypnosis). First: you must believe that you can change your personality.

these situations in your mind. It could be your boss congratulating you for some work well done. It could be someone expressing his or her love for you, or complimenting you. You may recall winning a contest or some kind of competition. It may have been during the course of an evening with friends, when you made some hilarious remark or found the perfect repartee (as your confidence grows, you'll soon develop an ability to say the right thing at the right time). It could also be a moment of tenderness or intimacy with someone you love. What matters is that when you relive these moments you feel good, you feel important. And by reliving these moments you can reconstruct your self-confidence, since the subconscious, as we saw in Chapter 1, does not make any temporal distinctions.

In the second avenue of approach you will use the 'as if...'. You are going to visualize yourself in public situations, feeling at ease, smiling, surrounded by people who enjoy your company and appreciate what you have to say. You will imagine these situations in as much detail as possible - the setting, the people, exactly what is said and what goes on. You will visualize a host of such situations.

They may involve a man or woman whom you find attractive, but whom you haven't dared approach as yet. Imagine yourself with that person, enjoying a good meal, walking hand in hand through the park, and so on. Your loved one smiles, letting you know that the feeling of love is reciprocal. And you feel completely confident. You spontaneously come up with the right thing to say, and your partner finds you charming and witty. Your gestures are perfect, you are tender and romantic. You imagine the situation as if you have already been lovers for a long time. The results will amaze you. The power of thought will work its magic, not only on you, but on the people around you as well.

An Example

You can resort to this technique for any situation which requires confident action. Say you have to make a speech in front of a group of people for the first time in your life. Just the thought of it terrifies you. Your throat gets dry, your hands are moist with perspiration. Imagine yourself making the speech, confronting your audience.

Once again, visualize the scene in as much detail as possible. Create an ideal situation, with yourself as the star performer. People start by giving you a warm round of applause as you make your entrance. A joke comes to mind, and through your sense of humor you immediately win over your audience. You have prepared your notes carefully, but you don't really need them and lay them aside. You know your text. Frequent bursts of applause punctuate your delivery. When it's over, you get a standing ovation and people rush up to congratulate you.

You see, it's simple. Of course, I can't provide examples for every possible situation. But you can. Just create a positive scene that meets your requirements.

Imagine the perfect situation, and live it in advance as as it had already happened.

Your confidence level will multiply tenfold, and very often things will work out exactly as you imagined they would. One thing is certain: your increased confidence level will be apparent both to you and to those around you. And this is only the beginning. Each success will consolidate your newfound confidence and make it grow even stronger.

HOW TO CREATE A NEW PERSONALITY

Anyone can do it, on two conditions (and these conditions apply to all applications of self-hypnosis). First: you must believe that you can change your personality.

these situations in your mind. It could be your boss congratulating you for some work well done. It could be someone expressing his or her love for you, or complimenting you. You may recall winning a contest or some kind of competition. It may have been during the course of an evening with friends, when you made some hilarious remark or found the perfect repartee (as your confidence grows, you'll soon develop an ability to say the right thing at the right time). It could also be a moment of tenderness or intimacy with someone you love. What matters is that when you relive these moments you feel good, you feel important. And by reliving these moments you can reconstruct your self-confidence, since the subconscious, as we saw in Chapter 1, does not make any temporal distinctions.

In the second avenue of approach you will use the 'as if...'. You are going to visualize yourself in public situations, feeling at ease, smiling, surrounded by people who enjoy your company and appreciate what you have to say. You will imagine these situations in as much detail as possible - the setting, the people, exactly what is said and what goes on. You will visualize a host of such situations.

They may involve a man or woman whom you find attractive, but whom you haven't dared approach as yet. Imagine yourself with that person, enjoying a good meal, walking hand in hand through the park, and so on. Your loved one smiles, letting you know that the feeling of love is reciprocal. And you feel completely confident. You spontaneously come up with the right thing to say, and your partner finds you charming and witty. Your gestures are perfect, you are tender and romantic. You imagine the situation as if you have already been lovers for a long time. The results will amaze you. The power of thought will work its magic, not only on you, but on the people around you as well.

An Example

You can resort to this technique for any situation which requires confident action. Say you have to make a speech in front of a group of people for the first time in your life. Just the thought of it terrifies you. Your throat gets dry, your hands are moist with perspiration. Imagine yourself making the speech, confronting your audience.

Once again, visualize the scene in as much detail as possible. Create an ideal situation, with yourself as the star performer. People start by giving you a warm round of applause as you make your entrance. A joke comes to mind, and through your sense of humor you immediately win over your audience. You have prepared your notes carefully, but you don't really need them and lay them aside. You know your text. Frequent bursts of applause punctuate your delivery. When it's over, you get a standing ovation and people rush up to congratulate you.

You see, it's simple. Of course, I can't provide examples for every possible situation. But you can. Just create a positive scene that meets your requirements.

Imagine the perfect situation, and live it in advance as as it had already happened.

Your confidence level will multiply tenfold, and very often things will work out exactly as you imagined they would. One thing is certain: your increased confidence level will be apparent both to you and to those around you. And this is only the beginning. Each success will consolidate your newfound confidence and make it grow even stronger.

HOW TO CREATE A NEW PERSONALITY

Anyone can do it, on two conditions (and these conditions apply to all applications of self-hypnosis). First: you must believe that you can change your personality.

The first condition for success is to believe that you can change your personality

But I'm fairly certain that you've already been persuaded of that. The second condition is that you must sincerely desire a change.

To transform your personality you must sincerely desire a change

If not, there's no point trying to use the method. If, for example, you only have a vague, half-hearted and passing desire to transform yourself, you probably won't succeed. This said, self-hypnosis can help you define your goals since it helps you see to yourself more clearly and to strengthen your willpower. This is because you are not depending solely on your conscious will (which is usually rather weak) for guidance, but can also draw on the tremendous power of your subconscious - in fact, of your entire being - to achieve your purpose.

Create Your Ideal Self-portrait

Once these two basic requirements are met, you are ready to begin work on your new personality. But there's still something you have to do, something very important. You have to create a profile of the ideal person you secretly wish you could become.

The best thing to do is to take a pencil and paper and write a list of the qualities you would like to acquire and the faults you want to eliminate (emphasizing the qualities rather than the faults). Don't hold back - you will be the only person to read this list. After using it you will destroy it. Writing down what you think is important because it helps to confirm your intentions and to clarify what you want.

Draw up your suggestion-formulations in accordance with this list. Use the technique of mental cinema to create scenes in which you possess the qualities you desire. Success will follow, you can be certain. But first you have to dream a little.

Model your personality however you wish. It has already been modeled in the past, without your knowing it, and in a way that displeases you, or which you at least do not find completely satisfactory. Now it's your turn to take charge. You are going to clean the slate of all your faults, and redesign yourself the way you want to be.

Tell yourself that, no matter what your present state is, no matter what deficiencies of character you now suffer from, no matter how many times you have failed in the past, you can change. Remember the story of Demosthenes. When he was young, he stuttered. Yet, through determination and perseverance, he was able to become one of the greatest orators of ancient Greece. To cure himself of his terrible affliction, Demosthenes put stones in his mouth and practiced speaking. He would wander along the deserted beaches of Greece, declaiming tirades that would later make him famous, gaining confidence in the power of his mind and his ability to overcome his natural handicap.

Compared to Demosthenes, you are very lucky - you don't have to wander over deserted beaches with stones in your mouth! All you have to do is stretch out and relax, and let your imagination and your subconscious do the work.

If other methods have failed you up to now on a personal and professional level, self-hypnosis really is the solution. When applied correctly, and practiced assiduously, it is an infallible method.

HOW TO INFLUENCE OTHERS AND BECOME A LEADER

Everyone wants to improve their public relations and be able to influence others.

That is a perfectly legitimate goal. Skill in maintaining good human relations is a guarantee of success. Why? For a very simple reason, that we nevertheless often tend to forget. When we say that we've made a deal with such and such a company, or an organization like a bank, we are really only telling a half-truth and, in a certain way we are actually lying to ourselves. Because when we make a deal, it's always with an individual and not with some anonymous entity like a 'company'.

It is other people who can help us to get what we want. It is a person who can open a door for you, who can agree to give you a loan, who decides to give you promotion, who is willing to refund your money when you're not satisfied with a purchase. And of course in your personal relationships - with friends and family - you're always dealing with people. People who are separate and different from you, who have their own problems, ambitions and dreams. Just like you. Unfortunately, this is another fact we often forget. 'An egotist,' George Bernard Shaw once said in jest, 'is anyone who continually refuses to think about my pleasure.' Remember that maxim when you want someone to like you, so that you can influence that person and obtain what you want.

You have to be sincerely interested in other people. Listen when they speak to you. Try to determine their needs, their ambitions. Put yourself in their shoes.

That's the best way to get to know someone, so that you can do something for him or her. Smile. Cultivate the art of making compliments. People will start flocking to you like bees to honey. Be sincere, and try to help people whenever you can.

And above all, learn to be yourself. It's all very well to want to please others. But you mustn't be afraid to displease people either, if the situation requires it.

I have the right to say no to someone without losing his or her love or respect
Others can say no to me without it affecting me

You're an adult, so you might as well act like one. Be spontaneous and express yourself. That's right, be yourself. Don't be afraid to express your opinions or ideas.

I have confidence in myself and in life, and I instill confidence in others

But above all, learn the art of developing a magnetic personality. Then you will inspire the people around you with your natural sense of authority. They'll listen when you speak, and they'll actually want you to influence them. Your simplest desires will exert considerable influence because of your increased power. But what is the key to acquiring a magnetic personality? Making use of the power of your subconscious and allowing the incredible energy, which you've kept trapped inside you up until now, to shine free, illuminating both your own person and the people around you.

That is the real secret of what we call charisma. Some people seem naturally endowed with this superior form of charm, but most people who possess it have developed it, and so can you.

When you do, you will become a natural leader, even if that is not your intention.

People will trust you, they'll enjoy working with you and for you. You will be entrusted with more important and more interesting responsibilities. Here is the method. Once again, there are two approaches, verbal and visual.

Verbal Formulation

'My personality is becoming more and more magnetic. I am able to influence the people around me at will.'

Variation: 'People are more and more attracted to me. I please everyone I meet.'

Visual Formulation

You can create a situation where you are surrounded by people who listen religiously to what you have to say, or regard you with admiration... Alternatively (and this technique is very powerful for developing charisma since it coincides with the occult definition of 'aura'), you imagine a golden light radiating out from around your head, like a halo, illuminating the people around you. It is a light of joy, peace, love and harmony.

The more you practice self-hypnotic relaxation, the more you liberate your real self, the more you emanate this invisible, but very real light, and the more you will influence the people around you. You will become their haven of peace and joy.

People will instinctively seek out your company.

Here is a very effective variation of the visual method for situations where you are confronted with a specific problem and wish to influence someone in a particular way. I have often used it myself, with much success. The technique is that of mental cinema. You imagine the situation you want to happen as if it has already happened, and with the person you want to influence acting as you want him or her to act.

Here's a personal example. One day, before I had set up my own company, one of the directors of the company I was working for came to my office and told me about a decision he had made without consulting me. I found the decision unreasonable, but before I could express my views or defend my point of view the director left, leaving me to carry out a task I considered absurd, and contrary to the interests of the company. It was an ideal occasion to apply the method of influencing someone indirectly.

I didn't get upset. That night, in the privacy of my own bedroom, I stretched out, relaxed, and induced the state of self-hypnosis. Then I imagined the following scene. The next morning, the director arrives and explains that he has changed his mind, that he has found a better solution, and that we are going to use such-and- such a strategy instead of the original decision. I then had him dictate my own solution as if it were his own, making sure not to leave out any details. I heard the sound of his voice, and I visualized everything as clearly as I could. I reinforced my visualization by repeating the following formulation: 'Tomorrow, Mr. X will tell me he has changed his mind.'

The next day, the director in question did not come to my office as I had predicted (or at least hoped) he would. I was extremely disappointed. But I was wrong to feel let down, because a little later on I noticed, right there on a corner of my desk, a memo I had overlooked. It was an internal memo from this director, and on it was the text I had mentally suggested the night before, almost word for word!

I could cite dozens of similar cases. You may have heard of some yourself, since most people can, to varying degrees, unconsciously exert this kind of indirect influence. The difference is that you can now do it consciously, under any circumstances that might arise. You might want a certain job offer or an invitation to some function. You certainly wouldn't mind a rise in salary, especially if you don't have to ask for it (it is possible!). It's up to you to explore all the avenues, and they are infinite.

One word of caution: as you develop your inner power, you will soon be able to start influencing the people around you, in whatever way you want, either for their benefit or for their harm. So be careful.

Remember the 'law of return' I mentioned earlier. All the harm we do will surely come back to us. So when you exercise your personal influence, make sure you adhere to the golden rule: Never do unto others what you would not have them do unto you.

In any case, I wouldn't worry about it too much. People who practice hypnosis generally develop a generous and beneficent disposition as a kind of side effect.

That's perfectly normal. You feel more balanced, more at peace with yourself; in short, happier. Your influence will therefore probably be beneficial.

SUMMARY OF CHAPTER 3

- Your success depends on your personality. Your personality is what you think you are. It is defined by your limitations and by your mental self- image.
- To overcome a lack of self-confidence, as well as other types of complexes, use the suggestion: 'Day by day, in every way, I am getting stronger and more and more confident.'
- Recreate moments of happiness and success in your mind. Imagine yourself as you would like to be. Use the 'as if' technique to imagine yourself in positive situations.
- The first condition for success is believing that you can change your personality. To transform your personality, you must also sincerely want to change.
- Look at things from other people's perspective. Learn to say no. Tell yourself: 'My personality is becoming more and more magnetic. I can influence the people around me as I want.'
- Use the 'golden light' technique.
- Make sure you use your influence to benefit others.

4

GET HEALTHY AND STAY HEALTHY

The Origin of Disease

Heredity is certainly a determining factor in the health of an individual. But it isn't the only factor. Even unfortunate genetic problems can often be overcome. In fact, you can build (or rebuild) your health, which is something you need to succeed in life fully. And through self-hypnosis, you can do a lot more than that.

This method will not only help cure your body of most illnesses and improve your resistance to most diseases, it will also help you discover a new sense of physical plenitude, a feeling which is not simply the result of an absence of illness but an affirmation of radiant health.

These days, even people in so-called 'good health' are usually not bursting with energy. Health is defined from a negative point of view-being healthy means not being ill. That's fine, of course. But we have to go a little further.

Anyone, regardless of his or her present state of health, can discover the secret of 'positive health'. Why? Because, contrary to what most people think, the origin of most illnesses is not physical. The illness may manifest itself physically, but the body is not its source. In scientific circles, the psychosomatic factor is being more and more accepted as a major cause of illness. Researchers at the Mayo Clinic in

Rochester, USA, estimate that 80 per cent of our illnesses originate in this way. Let me remind you of the Greek origin of the word 'psychosomatic', so that we can reflect on it for a moment together. It comes from the words psyche, which means mind, and soma, which means body.

The meaning is simple - so simple that it is often overlooked as a factor in a host of disorders such as asthma, allergies, heart problems, skin problems and enuresis.

Psychosomatic illnesses start in the mind before appearing in the body.

This is worthy of some reflection, for the simple reason that if we can exert a favorable influence on our mind before an illness manifests itself physically, and if that influence were completely effective all the time, we could prevent almost all illnesses. Perhaps you're a little skeptical. On the other hand, if you're sensitive to your body's needs, and especially if you're attentive to the periods that precede illness, you'll know what I'm talking about. Let me give you some examples.

HOW TO OVERCOME DISEASE

Very often, an illness's incubation period is characterized by sadness, stress, fatigue and so on. This follows some setback or disappointment, or represents a need to attract attention (or rather the affection of the people around you), a need to withdraw from the world, or even a need to inflict self-punishment because of some feeling of guilt. The problem is that we often confuse cause and effect. We think that the depression which precedes an illness is the first symptom of that illness, while in reality it is the cause.

This may seem surprising, and even paradoxical. But try to remember the last time you were ill. If you can clearly recall how the illness began, you may be in for a surprise. Don't people very often start to feel unwell after receiving some bad news? Think about what happens when someone is made redundant, or has to accept the lose of a loved one, or finds their work too difficult. They become ill.

And what made them ill? Words, simple words.

- 'We must unfortunately inform you that we no longer require your services. You are being laid off.'

Or

- 'I'm leaving you .... '

Of course, these words will be translated into facts and concrete situations. They will have unpleasant consequences, they can cause problems, sadness, even passionate drama. But in such cases, the illness that follows results directly from the emotional shock, from stress whose origin has nothing to do with a virus or microbe (which, however, does not mean that the physical illness will not be of a viral or otherwise infectious nature). The body, guided by a troubled mind, will accept and even attract the virus it needs to translate its mental symptoms into physical ones. This is just another illustration, albeit a spectacular one since it has physical repercussions, of the law of return (you reap what you sow). An accepted imbalance of the mind will always have physical repercussions.

THE REAL ORIGIN OF DISEASE IS IN THE MIND

It is for this reason that we can say that a person who has a perfectly positive and balanced frame of mind will also enjoy perfect health and protection from all disease. Disease is negative and disharmonious. Health is the opposite - positive and harmonious.

Being perfectly positive means being perfectly healthy

This is an absolute law, with no exceptions. Of course, it isn't easy to develop a perfectly harmonious mind which never allows disease to take root. Nevertheless, as you will see a little later on, you can work towards achieving this goal.

But first I want to present some more examples to convince you of the importance of your state of mind where the origin of disease is concerned. The ones I have chosen illustrate how an illness can be caused by a simple suggestion, or the repetition of a suggestion, which is the same as conditioning or programming. I have already told you the story of the employee who came to work in the morning and was told by a number of colleagues that he didn't look well, and who subsequently fell ill, or at least really started to feel ill. There was also the case of the erroneous diagnosis, which was even more spectacular. Here's another, yet more dramatic example, reported by Dr Joseph Murphy.

HOW A SUGGESTION KILLED A MAN

A cousin of mine went to India and consulted a fortune teller who told him that he had a weak heart, and predicted he would die before the next new moon. He told his family about this, and prepared his will.

This powerful suggestion was able to take root in his subconscious because he accepted it completely. He told me that the fortuneteller he had consulted was reputed to possess strange occult powers that enabled him to help or harm people.

The man died as was predicted, without ever knowing the cause of his own death.

Most of us have heard similarly strange stories, just as superstitious and apparently ridiculous as this one. But let's analyze it in the light of our understanding of the way the subconscious works. Anything the conscious mind believes, the subconscious will accept, and act accordingly.

My cousin, at the time he consulted the fortuneteller, was a happy, healthy, vigorous and robust man, in the prime of life. The fortuneteller made a very negative suggestion, which my cousin accepted. He was terrified, and started constantly thinking about his impending death. He told everyone and prepared for it. He didn't have to do this - his actions were dictated by his own mind. It was his fear that caused his own death, or rather the destruction of his body. His fear and his expectation that he would die.

The fortuneteller who predicted his death had no more power than a stone or a log. His suggestion had no power in itself to cause the tragic end he predicted. If my cousin had been aware of the laws governing the mind, he could have completely rejected this negative suggestion, refused to pay any attention to the man's words, knowing in his heart that he was governed and controlled by his own thoughts and feelings, and not by anyone else. His suggestion would have been no more effective than an arrow hitting a nuclear submarine. The prophecy of death would have been completely neutralized, it would have dissolved into thin air, without harming my cousin.

As you can see, words - and nothing but words - killed this man. They formed a destructive suggestion, against which he should have defended himself, but didn't because of his. ignorance of the universal laws of the mind. In our day-to-day lives we often encounter similar (if less spectacular) examples that illustrate the same principle.

Here's another example. My grandmother died recently. She had always said she would live to at least ninety, but was very afraid of suffering or of not being able to take care of herself. She was haunted by this fear, and died on her ninetieth birthday from a massive stroke, while she was eating lunch. As you can see, she programmed her own death ....

HOW WE PROGRAM OURSELVES TO BE ILL

This may sound bizarre - is there anyone who actually wants to be ill? Well, more people than you think. But most of the time, the desire to be ill is unconscious. Let me tell you about a personal experience.

When I was very young, my health, although generally good, was not as strong as it is today (aware as I now am of the laws of self-healing, or of what I call 'mental prevention', which is the only way to true health as far as I'm concerned).

But when I was young, I don't know why - maybe it was because I fell ill two or three times in the early autumn - my mother would say, 'Oh, Christian always gets ill in September....' It was nothing serious, just a touch of flu, but enough to keep me in bed for a few days. But invariably, with the coming of autumn, I 'caught the flu'.

It took me a few years to realize that I had been unconsciously programmed to get ill in September, in order not to disappoint my mother - in order to fulfill her expectation. As soon as I understood this the spell was broken- I shattered my program of sickness.

THE GREAT SECRET OF SELF-HEALING

I hope you are now convinced of the importance of the mind in the development of disease. Did you know that some of the more avant-garde researchers are starting to think that even cancer (the greatest scourge of the twentieth century and one for which a cure has not yet been found) originates in the mind? An analysis of thousands of people suffering from this terrible affliction has demonstrated that in almost all cases the initial physical symptoms were preceded by serious depression, melancholy, or a powerful and persistent wish to die. It seems as if the future patient's subconscious mind literally orders his or her body to become seriously ill, thereby succumbing to the desire for death. As we have seen, the subconscious obeys blindly, and with tremendous force, indifferent to whether its effects are beneficial or harmful.

One of the first people to make the connection between the subconscious and the development of disease was Emile Coué, the French pharmacist who became famous for his theories on positive suggestion (p. 34). He made his discovery by accident. A customer came to the pharmacy and asked for some medication that required a doctor's prescription, which he didn't have. Coué refused, saying that without a prescription he'd be breaking the law. But the customer persisted, begging for the medication. Coué, realizing that the illness was not serious but that the customer was, pretended to acquiesce. But in fact he only gave the man sugar pills.

A short time later the customer returned, overjoyed, and announced that he was completely cured. This is a typical case of what is called the 'placebo effect'. It appears that what cured the patient was his belief that the medication would work.

This belief, although false, was accepted by his conscious mind and recorded in his subconscious, which then acted accordingly and ordered the body to heal itself.

There is no better example of the curative power of self-hypnosis.

Now here is some valuable advice on how to use the great secret of self-healing - which, incidentally, has been known under various names by many cultures since the dawn of time. To start with, you must constantly cultivate thoughts of health.

Health, like happiness, is first and foremost a mental habit. Think healthy. If you are ill, don't name your illness. Don't talk about it. Remember the law of attraction: you will attract the effects which correspond to the causes you have created in your mind. If you think about being ill, you will become ill. Many people maintain an attitude of illness in their minds (and consequently in their bodies) by constantly talking about their ailments, analyzing them, complaining about them and comparing them. Their illness becomes their reason for living, so to speak, their entertainment and principal subject of concern. Nothing could be more harmful to health.

GET RID OF DISEASE THROUGH THE POWER OF YOUR MIND

We often get ill out of habit. We accept the idea of illness, which we judge to be a normal state, at least on occasions. However, the real normal state, and your right as a human being, is health: constant and flourishing good health.

> **Accepting the idea of sickness means you are already sick**
> **Good health is your absolute right**
> **Use it**

Under no circumstances should you allow thoughts of illness to enter your mind, whether they come from you or from someone else. Take time out to do a little self-analysis, as we have done on a couple of occasions already. Are you already programmed to become ill? Do you get ill every winter, because for years you've been unconsciously repeating to yourself something like, 'I don't know why, but every winter I catch a cold'?

Even if you complain about getting ill and say you don't understand why you do, your conscious mind accepts it as a kind of fatal destiny and your subconscious mind registers it as such. If you suffer from this kind of cyclical illness, look to your mind for the cause. It might be something that occurred in the distant past.

But it doesn't matter. You can reprogram yourself. You'll see exactly how in a moment.

Listen to your body, and to its inner state. Earlier I enumerated a number of situations which lead directly to disease. I advise you to be very careful as soon as any of the following situations arise:

- A personal let-down
- Losing your job
- Changing jobs
- Divorce or relationship break-up
- Loss of a child
- Illness of a loved one
- Moving house
- Losing a large sum of money
- Having to pay back a large debt
- Death of a parent or dose relative

All these situations can lead to disease. If and when they occur, defend yourself.

You will have to saturate your subconscious with positive and opposite suggestions. Apply the law of substitution that you have already learnt: immediately replace thoughts of disease with thoughts of health.

HOW TO REACT IN ORDER TO GET RID OF AN ILLNESS RIGHT FROM THE START

Incidentally, traumatic situations are not the only cause of disease. There's also the accumulation of daily worries, problems, minor disappointments and, of course, Public Enemy No.1 -stress.

Listen to your body. You may have noticed that you often receive a presentiment that you will get ill just before it happens. You say to yourself, 'I feel like I'm getting ill.' This is the time to react. Don't wait another instant. You immediately have to start reprogramming yourself.

I'm now going to give you some general formulations for health that can be used at any time. Later on, I'll be giving you more specific formulations for different types of ailments. These formulations have a powerful preventative effect. They can also be applied when you are already ill, and are trying to get better. The style of formulation is the same as I gave earlier.

One of the most effective formulations, which is at the same time very easy to remember, is the equivalent of the success-wealth formulation (p. 31). It states simply: strength-health. Repeat these two words endlessly in your mind and aloud.

Record them. Write them down. They are your passport to health.

STRENGTH - HEALTH

Here are some other formulations:

Every cell and every tissue in my body is regaining complete health and harmony

Every day I create positive and harmonious thoughts and emotions

They are transforming my life and bringing me happiness and health

My health is improving daily

I am becoming radiantly healthy

I breathe harmony, strength and health

My strength and health are improving daily

I love my body

I have the power to heal myself

The power of my subconscious heals my body and assures me of perfect health

Ask Your Subconscious for the Cure to Your Health Problem

We have already discussed the technique of setting up a dialogue with your subconscious. Your subconscious knows everything about you; therefore it also knows about your illness. So at night, before going to sleep, ask your subconscious why you are ill. And order it to indicate a remedy.

By this I don't mean that you should replace your doctor with your subconscious.

It's always best to consult a doctor, even before practicing self-healing. You want to take every precaution you can. The problem is that doctors are often incapable of curing disorders of psychosomatic origin, such as migraine, stomach ulcers, arthritis, backaches, skin problems and so on.

This is where the marvelous science of self-healing can come to your aid.

Let's get back to the subconscious. It will almost always provide you with a solution to your problem. You may be eating a certain food which is harmful to your system. You discover it by accident, while reading a magazine or talking to a friend. Or you may have a flash of intuition about it. But you can be sure that it is your subconscious talking to you.

HEALING IMAGES

You have just seen a few verbal formulations. Now let's look at the visual approach. You can use the mental cinema technique. Lying comfortably on your back, imagine yourself radiating good health. Strength and light emanate from all parts of your body. There's a smile on your face. You are in perfect health.

You can also create a variation of the technique used by the famous German poet Goethe, who imagined a close friend coming up to him and saying something positive. To improve your health, imagine your friend saying:

- 'You look in such great shape. How do you do it?'
- 'You look so healthy. I'm really impressed.'

Or

- 'I can't help but envy your fantastic health. What's your secret?'

In all your creative visualization sessions, support your images with repeated verbal formulations, and thoughts of balance and strength.

THE SUN TECHNIQUE

Another visualization, and a very powerful one, is called the sun technique. The sun is one of the most powerful and natural symbols of health and it's also a natural remedy. Imagine a sun in place of your heart. The heat of its rays spreads through your entire body. You are bathed in its light and warmth, as if you were on a beach in the tropics. Rays of strength and health emanate from your heart, radiating a great distance all around you. You are the sun. You absorb its strength through your heart and then radiate it, multiplying it a thousand fold. Your inner sun becomes as strong as the sun in the sky. It is just as powerful, and endows you with perfect health.

A variation of the sun technique, which is in fact very ancient, is the golden sphere. I personally find it extremely effective, and practice it regularly. We have already seen it used in the section on relaxation. Imagine a sphere of golden light surrounding your entire body. Its light penetrates all your limbs, which become luminous and light, filled with renewed energy. Your whole body pulses with magnetic energy, and your skin glows.

EMILE COUÉ'S HEALING METHOD

This method is very simple. There's nothing new about it- there are references to it in many ancient texts including the Bible. In fact, this was the method used by Jesus Christ himself, and a number of healers still use it today. It's called the 'laying on of hands'. Coué's method is a variation. Here's what he has to say, and I believe his simple language describes his method to perfection:

Every time, during the course of a day, that you experience some physical or mental suffering, affirm to yourself immediately that you will get rid of it. Then isolate yourself as much as possible, close your eyes and, laying your hand on your forehead (if the problem is mental!) or on the affected part of your body (if the problem is physical), repeat these words as quickly as possible: 'It's going away, it's going away, it's going away...' etc. for as long as it takes for the pain to pass.

With a little practice, you can get rid of almost any kind of physical or mental pain in about 20 seconds. Do the exercise each time the pain occurs.

HOW TO COMBAT NERVOUS FATIGUE AND OVERCOME INSOMNIA

There are two types of fatigue. There's normal fatigue, which we call healthy fatigue, and which results from physical effort like walking in the countryside, or spending a day on the ski slopes, or doing some manual labor.

The other kind of fatigue, called nervous fatigue, is really an illness.

Unfortunately, many people these days suffer from it. It is mainly caused by stress - which, incidentally, is the cause of a host of disorders. It is this kind of fatigue that prevents people from sleeping, for example, when they say they are 'overtired'.

It's this kind of fatigue that makes you feel tired when you get up in the morning, even after eight hours of sleep.

Self-hypnosis will help you get rid of this negative fatigue -which is not normal, even if you've got used to it. It has become so common these days that it can be considered one of the plagues of the twentieth century.

It's time you got rid of your chronic fatigue once and for all. Your sessions of relaxation will have already done a lot to cure the problem. Here are a few formulations specifically designed to combat fatigue. The best time to repeat them is at night, before falling asleep.

I sleep in order to fulfill my desires

Every night brings me deep, replenishing sleep

I awaken every morning full of joy and confidence

I am developing more and more energy and strength

Insomnia, of course, is one of the main causes of nervous fatigue. There are two forms of insomnia.

The first form is simply that you have a problem getting to sleep at night, or that you wake up a number of times during the night and can't get back to sleep. Both of these make it difficult to get through the following day and, if the insomnia is chronic, will eventually result in a state of nervous fatigue.

The second form of insomnia is more insidious. You fall asleep (more or less easily), but are never able to attain deep sleep, which is the state in which you renew your energy. You're half-asleep, instead of really sleeping deeply. You wake often, but not for long, and then fall into half-sleep again. In the morning you are often tired and irritable, as if you hadn't slept at all.

For both types, I advise verbal formulations. One of the simplest and most effective, which I suggest you try first, is the following (it's best to do it when you are already in bed, for obvious reasons). As you breathe in deeply, mentally repeat the following:

- 'Sleep... sleep ....'

And then as you exhale:

- 'Sleep deeply... sleep deeply ....'

Usually, repeating the suggestion 20 times is enough. If you don't drop off right away, you probably will after a few minutes. Then you will enjoy a deep and recuperative sleep.

Another technique which is equally effective, as you will see, is one I described earlier for inducing a state of self-hypnosis.

My eyes are getting tired, very tired. Soon my eyelids will be so heavy I'll have to close my eyes, and sleep will come. My body feels more and more relaxed. I am getting sleepier and sleepier, sleepier and sleepier, sleepier and sleepier. I'm now going to start a long, slow countdown (a hundred down to zero). The more I count, the sleepier I get. I am gradually falling into a deep sleep, deeper and deeper.

Soon I'll lose track of the numbers and I'll be deeply asleep. I'll fall into a deep and replenishing sleep. I'll sleep all night long without awakening, and in the morning I will wake up perfectly rested and full of energy.

After a few days of this you'll feel regenerated and bursting with energy. Don't forget that sleep is the best medicine there is, as long as it is deep sleep. Insomnia will no longer be a problem for you, and you will experience just how revitalizing deep sleep can be.

As a result, you'll probably need less sleep than you did before, and you'll be able to save up to two hours a day. That's two more hours in which to be happy, to enjoy life, to work towards your success and to help others succeed. And those extra two hours will be much more productive and efficient. So goodnight and sweet dreams!

HOW TO GET RID OF PAIN AT WILL

The therapeutic possibilities of self-hypnosis are amazing. However, I just want to repeat what I said earlier - self-hypnosis is not a substitute for your doctor. It can help him or her to help you, by acting as a complement to the medical treatment you are receiving. This is important to remember, especially when using the method to anaesthetize some part of the body. Pain is a signal. Your body uses it to warn you of potential danger (placing your hand on a burning object) or of some malfunction (disease).

Pain is also a way for your mind to 'somatize' (in other words, to translate into physical language) your mental tensions, frustrations and disappointments. And this is precisely the area in which self-hypnosis has its greatest effect.

In some instances self-hypnosis is the perfect way to get rid of pain - sometimes it can even be your only choice. For example, say you cut your hand and the pain is severe. There's no doctor in the vicinity- you're out walking in the forest. It'll take you at least an hour to walk to the nearest town. What can you do? Well, you can anaesthetize your pain. The best way to do it is for a predetermined period of time - for example, for the hour it will take you to reach help.

Relax, and enter the state of self-hypnosis. Then repeat the following formulations while concentrating on your injured hand:

Now all the pain in my hand is disappearing, and the blood is clotting quickly.

My pain is rapidly diminishing. I won't feel it at all for the next hour. It will disappear completely. I am now going to count to five. On the count of five, my pain will completely disappear, and I won't feel any pain for an hour (or whatever the desired period of time). One... two ...three... four... five ....

TOOTHACHE

This is an organic problem, which means that it does not have psychological causes. It is a symptom of tooth decay or some other kind of infection. Your must see a dentist. However, getting an appointment may take some time, and even in an emergency you may have to wait some hours or even days. So to avoid needless suffering while you're waiting, why not put yourself into a state of self-hypnosis?

Use the same formulation as in the preceding example, replacing the injured hand with your injured tooth.

As you can see, this technique can be used for numerous types of pain. You'll be amazed at how effective it is. You've probably heard about hypnotists who can produce sensations of extreme heat or cold in subjects just by making a simple suggestion. The same kind of force is used here, but in the opposite way. Here you want to suppress a sensation instead of creating one, in order to ease the pain you are suffering.

SUBSTITUTION TECHNIQUE FOR DEALING WITH PAIN

Use the power of images and a technique called 'sensorial substitution'. You start by imagining a situation where you can no longer feel your hand (for example you're out skiing on an extremely cold day, and you lose a glove). Your hand is numb. Mentally repeat the formulation: 'All I have to do is touch [whatever other part of your body you like] for it to become numb.'

HOW TO EASE AN ATTACK OF ACUTE ARTHRITIS

You use the same technique, except that here, because the disorder is chronic, you probably won't be able to get rid of the pain completely. You can eliminate about 75 per cent of it, however, which makes the condition a lot more bearable.

However, I should add that many people who have persevered and worked on the problem regularly have been completely cured through self-hypnosis, since the cause of arthritis is often continual emotional stress.

Repeat the following suggestion, and do not name the illness:

My energy is circulating more and more freely through my entire body, which is becoming light and luminous. My pains are disappearing completely, because the marvelous force of my subconscious is healing me completely.

If your attacks are localized in a specific area, say your knees, you can accompany these suggestions with another exercise. Imagine that your blood circulation increases in the afflicted region. Blood pours into your knees, spreading soothing heat and dissolving your pain.

BEAUTIFUL SKIN

Having beautiful skin is certainly an advantage, since a face is a little like a visiting card. Anyone can have a beautiful complexion as long as certain rules, including dietary ones, are respected. Obviously a person who eats a lot of fat and junk food will probably not have good skin.

Your skin is a mirror, the reflection of your inner self. Your tensions, your frustrations and your disappointments can all be seen on your skin. To have healthy skin, you have to have a healthy soul. If you are calm and relaxed, you'll have beautiful skin. Here are some exercises that can help you acquire a healthy and beautiful complexion, starting with a formulation.

My skin is becoming more and more beautiful and radiant. My face glows with freshness and energy. My complexion is improving day by day, becoming as fresh as a rose. My skin seems younger every day, as it regains its freshness and vitality, its elasticity and its healthy glow.

CREATIVE VISUALIZATION EXERCISE

Imagine that you're lying at the foot of a gentle, cool waterfall. The sparkling water falls softly on to your face, refreshing it and washing away all its imperfections. Your skin becomes more and more soft and satin-smooth. You emerge from this bath completely cleansed, refreshed, with perfect, shining, radiantly healthy skin.

ELIMINATE MIGRAINES

Millions of people suffer from migraines daily. They take a couple of pills, drink some herbal tea and may be able to soothe the pain - until next time. The migraine is soon back, with its terrible, piercing pain.

Most migraines are of psychosomatic origin. And you have to treat the cause, as well as the symptom, if you want to get rid of the disorder permanently. Emotional stress is the most frequent cause. This can be due to problems at work or personal problems at home, setbacks, disappointments, boredom, placing excessive demands on yourself and so on. When the migraine occurs only occasionally, and is due to temporary stress, a single session of self-hypnosis is usually enough.

However, when the migraine becomes chronic it's best to precede self-hypnosis with some self-analysis, in order to discover the cause. Hold a dialogue with your subconscious. Ask it to reveal the cause of your migraines. This will do a lot to facilitate your treatment.

Here's a formulation to use:

My head is opening, becoming calm and light. My energy starts circulating normally in my head, eliminating tensions, and fatigue. My blood nourishes every cell of my brain, which is bathed in soft light. My head is relaxing completely.

VISUAL VARIATION

Imagine a band of metal squeezing your head. The metal is black, as black as your problems and tensions. You re going to get rid of this piece of metal, which is causing you so much pain, once and for all. Imagine the band of metal splitting open and the pressure slowly diminishing. As the ban opens more and more, you feel your tensions and your pain dissolve. Now you lift the band, the image of your pain, off your head completely and throw it far, far away. And at that precise moment, your head feels completely free and relaxed.

DIGEST YOUR FOOD WITH EASE

The stresses of modern life often have a negative effect on your stomach. Many people digest their meals badly. Either their digestion is sluggish, or they experience pain after eating, even though they may not have developed an ulcer as yet. Obviously, proper functioning of the digestive system is essential for good health. People who digest badly cannot nourish their bodies adequately. The body does not get all the nutrients it needs and you become fatigued, lacking in energy, melancholic or depressed.

Self-hypnosis can resolve this problem. But before giving you the techniques, here's some basic advice. In the Western world we generally eat too much and too quickly. If you want to digest well, start by chewing your food well. You should chew until the foods turns to liquid in your mouth. Don't forget that digestion begins in your mouth: saliva contains powerful enzymes that break down your food. And an interesting side effect, especially if you're trying to lose weight, is that the more slowly you eat, the less you have to consume. Your psychological hunger is satisfied sooner, and you will need to eat smaller quantities to satisfy your physiological hunger. Remember the saying, 'We dig our graves with our teeth.'

So eat slowly and frugally. And do a few sessions using the following formulation:

My stomach is functioning normally again. It has all the energy it needs to do its work and metabolize the food I eat. Now I am digesting more and more easily. I break down my food and digest it with ease. As I digest, I am relaxed and calm.

As you'll soon see when you start digesting your food properly, you won't produce needless quantifies of bile and you'll start feeling great again.

WHY CAN'T PEOPLE GET RID OF THEIR ALLERGIES?

Most people think that allergies are hereditary, and that, once acquired, they remain with you for the rest of your life, or can at best be treated with regular injections. It is true that such injections are often effective, but they only ease the symptoms of allergies, and do nothing to eliminate the cause.

The cause of most allergies is psychosomatic. Many people become allergic after suffering some kind of trauma, which in turn creates a negative program in their subconscious. When a similar situation arises, the program produces the same reaction and the allergies start acting up again.

A child, for instance, may get bitten by a dog, a very traumatic experience that creates a program in the child's subconscious mind. When the child becomes an adult, he or she experiences severe and irrepressible skin eruptions on every contact with a dog. The person may not even remember the original incident. But the subconscious mind never forgets.

This is only one example among a host of other possibilities. Some people are allergic to pollen, others to the fur of certain animals and yet others to dust, to certain odors, to grass, to particular foods and so on. A few sessions of self- hypnosis are usually sufficient to treat an allergy. Sometimes even a single session will do the trick, especially if the person is used to inducing a state of hypnotic relaxation. And often some self-analysis can help resolve the symptoms.

VERBAL/VISUAL HEALING METHOD

Formulation for food allergies:

I can now eat [such and such] food easily and with pleasure.- I am free of the negative influences of the past. My body now reacts normally to any food I absorb.'

As a visual variation, imagine yourself taking pleasure in eating the food to which you're allergic.

Formulation for animal allergies such as cats:

I find it more and more enjoyable to be with cats. Cats are gentle and lovable animals. My body reacts completely normally when I'm with cats.

As a visual variation, imagine yourself petting a cat that purrs with pleasure. You are smiling and relaxed, and you're completely rid of your allergy, which is only a memory of the past. It is even better to have the cat standing at some distance from you and then to visualize yourself approaching the animal without suffering any unpleasant allergic effects.

GENERAL METHOD

No matter what kind of allergy you have, you now know how to build a positive suggestion. It's a good idea to visualize a scene that corresponds to your formulation. This will reinforce your suggestion. Visualize yourself in a situation that usually brings on an allergic reaction, but imagine yourself relaxed, calm and without any allergic symptoms whatsoever.

HOW TO OVERCOME ASTHMA

In some ways, asthma can be classified as a form of allergy. However, people often have asthma attacks without being exposed to any allergy-causing element like pollen or animals. The attacks occur for no apparent reason. However, in reality there always is a cause, although it might not be exterior. With asthma, the cause is almost always psychological. An asthma attack, which is characterized by the spasmodic contractions of the bronchi, is usually the result of some anxiety or of excessive nervous tension. It could be said that asthma sufferers 'suffocate' from too much emotion.

Studies have shown that in most cases asthma is not hereditary. It is more like a physical reaction that becomes a habit as it is repeated. In other words, it becomes a subconscious program. Every time a patient has an attack, the program is reinforced. Self-hypnosis, as you can see, is an ideal treatment for asthma, since the best way to get rid of the problem is to change the program. Here is a suitable formulation:

I am becoming more and more relaxed every day. I feel liberated, and I react normally to any situation. I breathe deeply, filling my lungs, which are always free of obstruction. I can easily overcome my tension and anxiety. I can control all my bodily reactions perfectly. My bronchial tubes and my lungs are strong and relaxed. I breathe calmly and deeply under any circumstances. I always stay calm, and I control the way my body reacts. I feel more and more confident and relaxed, in all situations.

HOW TO RELIEVE BACKACHES

Backache can affect us all at some time or another. Here is a formulation to beat it:

All the muscles in my back are relaxing. The tensions in my back are dissolving completely. My whole back feels better and better. And my posture is improving at the same time. My spine is relaxing. My back is getting stronger day by day, as it is freed of all its tension.

At the same time, concentrate on the part of your back that hurts. Imagine your body temperature rising in the affected region. Blood flows in, replenishing the muscles and relaxing them. In general, after about four or five minutes you will really feel the warmth in your back and the pain will gradually diminish.

You can use the technique of raising your body temperature for any number of problems. It is very effective, and is especially recommended in cases of muscular pain. But don't forget that it takes a few minutes to start working, after which you will feel a real sensation of heat.

HELP FOR A STIFF NECK

I suggest using the same formulation as for your back. Simply replace the word 'back' with 'neck'. Use the temperature elevation method, which is especially effective for stiff necks.

OVERCOMING SEASICKNESS

Seasickness can be most unpleasant and a real nuisance when traveling. Try the following formulation:

I can travel on boats with ease. My body reacts completely normally, and I feel very balanced out on the ocean. I remain calm and relaxed, I digest my food perfectly normally, and I am in control of all my reactions.

I highly recommend doing some mental cinema for cases of seasickness, in order to reinforce your mental suggestions. Imagine yourself aboard a magnificent ocean liner. You are smiling and relaxed. You feel great, and contemplate the waves with no feelings of queasiness or distress. You experience no seasickness whatsoever - no nausea, no dizziness. Imagine yourself enjoying a good meal on board, laughing with friends, completely relaxed.

You can make your mental cinema sessions progressive: start with short trips around a bay, then go farther up the coast, then out on to the high seas and so on.

You can conclude your treatment by crossing the Atlantic!

COLDS AND SINUSITIS

When suffering from a cold or sinusitis, try using this formulation:

My breathing is now becoming easier and easier. I can breathe freely. My nose and sinuses are completely open. I can feel myself breathing well, and it makes me feel very good. All my respiratory passages are opening, and I can breathe freely.

Visualizing the golden sphere around your head will help get rid of a cold or sinusitis. Visualize the light as you repeat your verbal formulations.

HEART PROBLEMS

There are varying degrees of heart and circulatory problems. It's best, of course, to consult a doctor - this is especially important for cases involving the heart muscle itself. However, doctors don't have any magic formulas, and despite their reassurances that there's nothing seriously wrong, many people still don't feel very well. They may suffer from arrhythmia (irregular heartbeat), or experience sudden palpitations that can be somewhat painful and are always worrying. Or their pulse may be too fast, which gradually becomes extremely tiring since a lot of extra strain is put on the heart.

In such cases, it's a good idea to hold a dialogue with your subconscious. Heart problems often have a psychological cause. They can also be due to faulty diet or lifestyle: too much salt, coffee, cigarettes, alcohol and so on. Maybe a little more exercise would be appropriate, if there is no medical reason why you should not.

Whatever it is, your subconscious will inform you of it. Ask it for a solution to your particular problem and repeat the following formulation:

My heart is getting stronger and stronger, more and more calm, more and more relaxed. It beats slowly and regularly,' nourishing my entire body with fresh blood and oxygen. My heart is growing stronger day by day. It is becoming more and more calm and strong.

The rose technique can be used effectively as an accompaniment to these suggestions. I'll just repeat it quickly: you imagine a rose in place of your heart, a magnificent rose which opens its petals slowly, radiating strength, light and love.

You can also simply visualize your heart beating slowly and regularly.

Obviously there are many disorders that I have not been able to cover in this chapter. But now that you have grasped the basics of the technique, and seen it applied in a number of situations, you can adapt it to almost any situation that arises. Don't hesitate to do just that. Innovate. Discover new formulations. And don't forget: you can be the master of your own body and your health.

STRENGTH = HEALTH

SUMMARY OF CHAPTER 4

- Most illnesses begin in the mind, and are then translated into physical symptoms.
- Being perfectly positive means being perfectly healthy. Look for the origin of your disorder, and program yourself for health. Think of the equation: **Strength = Health**.
- Ask your subconscious for the remedy to your problem.
- Use healing images. Become a radiant sun of health.
- When you are suffering, repeat to yourself, 'It's going away, it's passing' and so on. Use positive formulations before going to sleep.
- Eliminate insomnia. Ease your pain at will, whether it's the

pain of a toothache or acute arthritis. Give yourself a satin-smooth complexion. Eliminate migraines and allergies, asthma and backaches, stiff necks, seasickness and heart problems. Digest your food with ease.
- This chapter contains images and formulations you can use to heal yourself.

5

CONTROLLING YOUR HABITS AND ADDICTIONS

A habit is second nature, as the saying goes - and nothing could be more true.

However, we must not forget that second nature is acquired. It is the result of a conditioning process, in other words of programming. There's no problem if all your habits are positive, of course. But if you develop bad habits (as everyone does), problems arise when you try to deal with them -when you try to change a negative aspect of your character. This is much easier said than done. We keep saying to ourselves, 'Come on, I have to do something about this!' or 'I'm going to make a real effort to get rid of this bad habit.' But as you've probably realized, even the best intentions are often futile.

A DIRECT EFFORT OF WILL IS USELESS

Willpower itself is usually not enough to get rid of a bad habit.

Yet we keep wanting to change. We try over and over again, using different methods, and end up resigning ourselves to the fact that 'it's stronger than I am'.

Do you know why? The answer lies in the law of inverse effect, formulated by Emile Coué at the turn of the 20th century, which states that: 'Whenever there is a conflict between imagination and willpower, imagination always wins.'

There's a celebrated illustration of this principle, called the 'plank story'. If someone asks you to walk along a plank lying on the ground, you will do so without any problem even if it is on a steep incline. But if you're asked to walk along the same plank, which is this time suspended 60 feet in the air, the feat will seem much more dangerous. The chances are that you'll refuse. You know it isn't difficult - you've just walked along the same plank when it was on the ground. So theoretically you know you can do it. You may even want to do it, but you just can't. Your imagination is stronger than your willpower. It is aware of the height of the plank, and you can already see yourself falling to the ground.

Self-hypnosis directly accesses the power of the subconscious, which is where all the programs resulting in bad habits are inscribed. For this reason, a session of self-hypnosis lasting a few minutes is usually worth hours of voluntary effort. You must address your subconscious directly, in its own language, which is quite different from the language you use to communicate with your conscious mind, and has proved ineffective up to now.

CONTROL YOUR WEIGHT WITHOUT DEPRIVING YOURSELF

Half the population of the Western world suffers from being overweight to some degree. You may be only a few pounds overweight, but you just can't seem to get rid of the excess fat. Or your problem may be more dramatic - you can develop serious health problems from carrying around too much excess weight. We see new books appearing on the shelves every week, offering miracle diets that guarantee weight loss 'in ten days or less'.

Many people have tried at least one of these miracle diets, and some have tried several. People deprive themselves, forcing themselves to adhere to a strict and frugal diet that their bodies are not used to, often for weeks on end. They do get results, but unfortunately these results are only temporary. A month later they've regained all their weight, and in many cases even gain some more. So they go out and look for another miracle diet, and the cycle begins all over again. This is a very happy situation for the booksellers and authors, but it doesn't do much for the people who are overweight.

WHY DO ALL THESE MIRACLE DIETS FAIL?

They fail because they don't deal with the real cause of obesity -bad nutritional habits. The only way to lose weight permanently is to break your bad habits and replace them with new ones. As I have just stated, habits originate in the subconscious. That's why, even though you may sincerely want to lose weight, even if you make a tremendous effort of willpower, you will fail without the participation of the subconscious. It's stronger than you are. You can't resist digging into a delicious Indian meal, or gorging yourself on cakes, again and again and again.

Being overweight is, therefore, the result of bad habits and not, as some people would like to believe, due to a malfunction of the metabolic system or of the thyroid gland. In fact, the real causes of obesity are psychological tension, sexual frustration, lack of affection, guilt complexes, boredom and so on. Food becomes a substitute, a compensation for whatever it is you are lacking. A vicious circle is established, where people become obese because they eat too much, and eat too much because they are obese, and develop a complex about being fat.

Unfortunately, the more that obese people eat to compensate for their problems, the more they reinforce the negative program recorded in their subconscious mind.

Fortunately, all is not lost. Bad habits can be broken, and a program for obesity can be changed. I am going to give you some incredibly effective formulations, which will help you regain your ideal weight without having to make any real effort or deprive yourself in any way. You won't have any trouble passing up a 450-calorie dessert, which you certainly don't need to stay healthy - and that, if anything, is actually harmful to your health. It will be easy because, once your new program is installed, you won't be the same person - you won't feel like a martyr as you refuse your portion of cream cake or chocolate pudding. Your subconscious will be programmed in such a way that you will feel absolutely no need for these kinds of foods, which are relatively useless in nutritional terms and do nothing to give you that happy, extremely pleasant feeling of having enjoyed a hearty and nutritious meal.

This is the magic of self-hypnosis. And it is for this reason that self-hypnosis is the only effective, lasting method for losing weight. And you won't have to make any effort at all. Your 'alimentary profile', if I may coin a phrase, will change completely.

RULES TO OBSERVE

There are, however, certain rules you must observe if your self-hypnosis program is to be successful. Before starting, talk to your doctor or to a dietitian, or consult a reputable book, and make a list of the foods you should eliminate from your diet or at least eat only infrequently. Also make a list of the foods you should eat.

Make a firm decision to lose weight. Ask your doctor to help establish your ideal weight. That will become your objective. Weigh yourself regularly in order to gauge your progress.

You must be convinced that you can easily lose weight through self-hypnosis.

Don't allow yourself to entertain any doubts. There's no question that you're not going to attain your ideal weight. Just be patient. It's better to lose weight gradually than all at once, which will only weaken your system. Think in ounces rather than pounds, especially if you've set a weekly goal for yourself. In any case, trust in the power of your subconscious. It knows exactly how fast you should lose weight, so that your goal is achieved in a balanced and healthy manner.

A minor note of caution: if you only want to lose a few pounds, there won't be any problem. But if you have a serious weight problem, you're probably better off carrying out your program of self-hypnosis under medical supervision. The two are in no way incompatible. Self-hypnosis is accepted as a valid form of treatment by the vast majority of doctors.

Before giving you the formulations you are going to repeat, allow me to reinforce your motivation a little more by telling you about some of the advantages you will enjoy after getting rid of your excess weight. Your appearance will improve, which in turn will make you more attractive to others, especially to the opposite sex.

You'll live longer, you'll be in better physical shape, you'll be more active and less tired, and your sex life will improve. You'll develop a new self-image, and you'll like yourself a lot more. So in a sense, losing weight can mark the beginning of success for the rest of your life!

Now the formulations:

I am gradually reaching my ideal weight, and will maintain it easily. My health is improving. My appearance is getting more and more attractive, and people are starting to seek out my company. I am improving day by day. I only eat healthy foods which allow me to lose weight easily, without depriving myself. I'm becoming more and more attractive and healthy, thanks to my subconscious. I can easily reach my ideal weight, and maintain it without effort. I like my body, and the new self-image I am creating through the power of my subconscious. I am in perfect control of my eating habits. I like my body, and I have the power to lose weight.

Choose the formulations you prefer. Don't hesitate to improve or embellish them.

Alternatively, record the complete text a number of times in succession, and listen to it during your daily session. I know you will succeed. And you'll come out a winner. Persevere until you achieve success.

A MENTAL IMAGE YOU CAN USE FOR SUPPORT

Visualize yourself as you would like to be, at your ideal weight. For example, you could be on the beach, wearing a sexy bathing suit. You're slim, attractive, vigorous and in perfect health. People of the opposite sex look at you with desire, and try to approach you. Those of your own sex are envious of your appearance.

You feel much, much better, you like your body... and so on.

STOP SMOKING IN TWO WEEKS

Nicotine is a poison. Cigarettes are dangerous to your health. It has been proven that smoking considerably shortens your lifespan. Most people afflicted with lung cancer were once heavy smokers. Cigarettes increase nervous tension, and can damage the heart and arteries. Smoke is bad for your complexion and for your eyes. Most smokers develop chronic bronchitis, which takes the form of the notorious 'smoker's cough'.

All smokers know this, and yet they continue to smoke. It's a habit, deeply rooted in their minds. There are two kinds of smokers: those who pretend to enjoy smoking and have no intention of stopping, and those who deplore the habit and would like to stop. Many people have tried to stop, and may have succeeded for a few days or weeks, or even for a few months. But then they start again. As George

Bernard Shaw once said, 'Oh yes, it's easy to stop smoking. I've done it dozens of times.' This second group of smokers want to stop but can't. The habit is stronger than they are, and they are slaves to it. Their willpower is powerless to help.

Now, in only two weeks, you can eliminate this harmful habit if you really want to. Start by making a clear and definite choice to do so, as with obesity. Also persuade yourself that the method is effective. Think about all the advantages of not smoking, and all the disadvantages of continuing.

Once you have entered the state of self-hypnosis, repeat the following formulations:

I can easily stop smoking. I am giving up the habit of smoking cigarettes completely. My health and general condition will improve at the same time. I can control the way I react to cigarettes. I have no desire to smoke. I am a new person, a person who bas no need for cigarettes. My subconscious is helping me to stop smoking with ease, once and for all, without gaining any weight.

Choose the formulations you prefer. Repeat them. Write them down. Write them on self-adhesive paper slips, and stick them up where you can see them. Do this to reinforce your determination. If you feel the need to smoke, chew gum or suck a sweet.

It takes about two weeks to stop smoking completely. Reduce the number of cigarettes you smoke each day. After a week, you should have reduced the number by at least half. Then as you approach the end of the two-week period, try to cut down to one or two cigarettes a day. You have almost attained your goal, but continue with your daily sessions in order to reinforce your new program. You'll still be tempted, but less and less frequently. And your need to smoke will be less intense. Your subconscious is now acting as a powerful ally. It is just as strong as when it prevented you from stopping smoking, only now it is working in the opposite sense - for you instead of against you.

After you've stopped smoking completely, reinforce your program by repeating:

I don't smoke any more. I bare stopped smoking, definitively and completely. My health bas greatly improved. I can breathe better, and I feel I'm in splendid shape.

Visual Technique

To reinforce your formulations, or as a substitute technique, visualize yourself putting out your last cigarette or breaking it in half and throwing away your last pack. Imagine yourself refusing a cigarette that someone offers you. You smile as you say, 'No thanks, I've given up.'

Or use this scenario. A friend comes up to you and says, 'Congratulations! I heard you'd stopped smoking. You look great. I think it's wonderful that you were able to give it up. It takes a lot of strength. I'm so glad you succeeded.'

HOW TO OVERCOME DEPRESSION AND REGAIN YOUR LOVE OF LIFE

Happiness is a habit, not some heaven-sent gift. Neither is being happy a question of luck, as many people believe. Think about it. Happiness is a habit, in the same way that smoking or drinking alcohol are habits. Except that being happy is a positive habit. In fact, it is the best habit you can acquire- and preserve. And when we talk about habits, we are talking about conditioning or programming.

The same applies to depression. It is the result of a negative program, often an extremely powerful one. But any program, as you now know, can be changed and replaced - even the worst kind of negative conditioning.

There are many exterior causes of depression: professional failure, a reversal of fortune, the loss of a loved one, a failed relationship, and so on. No one, even the most well balanced and positive of us, is immune to depression at some time in their life. That's fine as long as the state is temporary and not too severe. We aren't robots, so we can't always be radiantly happy (I'm not saying that a constant state of perfect happiness, or nirvana, is unattainable, but it does seem to be reserved for only a very few individuals).

But as well as this kind of minor, short-term depression, which positive people are able to overcome without much difficulty, there is the more serious type, which is called chronic depression.

People who suffer from chronic depression are all but paralyzed, incapable of functioning normally, apathetic, morose and so on. They may start crying on the slightest pretext, they have no appetite, and may even become anorexic. They say incomprehensible things, and often behave in bizarre, incoherent ways.

In cases where depression has become as serious as that, a doctor must be consulted. However, self-hypnosis can act as a powerful support to medical treatment, for the simple reason that depression is rarely of physiological origin (although it can be the result of a serious physical illness). Depression is referred to as a nervous disorder - in other words, it originates in the mind.

When diagnosing all forms of depression, even very serious cases, doctors and psychiatrists look for an event, or series of events, which brought on the disorder.

A person loses their job, for example, and the next day falls into a serious depression, proving that the cause is not physical but mental. Of course, it's never fun to lose your job. Even if you hate your work, loss of a job usually places a great strain on your finances, at least temporarily, especially if you have a family to take care of. But some people will continue on their way and overcome their difficulties, while others in the same situation will become seriously depressed and give up hope.

So in a manner of speaking it's not really the exterior circumstances which are the root cause of depression. The same cause produces radically different effects from person to person, a fact that is not in accordance with the law of universal causation. The determining factor, therefore, is not the event but the state of mind of the person - in other words, the person's mental programming.

In addition - and this very important- do you know why it is indispensable to maintain a positive frame of mind? It's not only because you are able to overcome obstacles, which are inherent to the human condition, more easily. It's because, in accordance with the law of mutual attraction, positive people attract other positive people, and create positive circumstances in their lives, which makes their task that much easier.

There's a proverb that goes, 'Only lend money to the rich.' In a way, the same applies to the mental level. If you are rich in ideas and spirit, if you are rich in happiness and positive thoughts, life will lend you more. It will make sure there is always an abundance of happiness in your life.

I am abundantly happy

Repeat this formulation. It's the best anti-depressant there is, since depression is the opposite of abundant happiness. Depression is the lack of happiness, of vitality.

When a person's mind is severely deprived of positive thoughts, life will not come to the rescue. Such a person's life is deprived of happiness.

Therefore happiness, like depression, is above all a state of mind. Let's get back to the example mentioned earlier: losing your job. Some people react badly and get depressed, having left the door open to extremely powerful negative suggestions (usually made by themselves). They suffer a mental breakdown and serious depression eventually sets in. They have succumbed to the very negative inner monologue described in Chapter 1. This is a continual and unconscious form of autosuggestion in which they repeat the message:

'This is serious. I lost my job.

What am I going to do? I'll never make it. I'll lose everything. I'll starve to death.

It'll take months to find another job, if I ever do. It's all over. I have no talent, I'm not competent enough to compete. That's why they made me redundant. I'm worthless...' and so on.

It's not the loss of the job that brings on the depression, but this kind of inner monologue - which the subconscious accepts, especially since it is charged with emotion. The depression is caused by the person's state of mind. And what is sad about such situations is that, as the person becomes depressed, he or she continually reinforces the negative program by continually thinking negative, pessimistic thoughts. It's a classic case of a vicious circle.

Our second job loser also has an inner monologue going. This person is disappointed, of course, but thinks something like: 'All right, I don't have a job. I have to react. I'll find another job this week. Anyway, it's not really that serious. A change of scene will do me good. And really, I didn't enjoy my work that much.

I've been feeling bored for a while now. [Remember that a person rarely gets fired from a job he or she really finds interesting and completely fulfilling. Usually, people who get laid off realize later on that the job they lost was not right for them, that they weren't evolving or learning anything, and that they should have left a long time before. We sometimes need a little 'kick in the butt' from life. But we should remember that things always work out for the best.] I am fully competent. I have experience. And luck is on my side. I know there's a job out there right now that is ideal for me. And I'm going to find it.'

I am thankful for everything that happens to me
There is a solution and I'm going to find it!

People who think this way will obviously not fall into a state of depression. They counter-attack by creating a positive program. You may say that it's easy for them, since they're already positive. And I agree, it is easier. But you too can become a positive person.

If you are severely depressed at the moment, I will only ask one thing of you, and that is to give my method a chance. It works a little like the French philosopher

Pascal's wager: If God exists, you have nothing to lose by believing in Him. If He exists, you will be saved. The same goes for my method. I am telling you this because, once the subconscious is negatively programmed in a certain direction (getting depressed, for example), that program will try to survive, to maintain itself, as if possessing a life of its own.

So a negative person will tend to reject any ideas that might help terminate the condition. The negative program would be threatened. It sends messages through your subconscious, telling you things like, 'It's useless even to try to solve this problem. Self-hypnosis doesn't work. You have to accept being unhappy. Life is like that...' and so on. To use a biological analogy, these negative thoughts are like antibodies secreted by the program to neutralize its aggressor, in this case your positive thoughts. The mechanism operates very subtly and usually unconsciously.

However, it will tenaciously resist being supplanted, like the devil, whose greatest trick is to get people to believe he doesn't exist. Then he can go ahead and do his dirty work, without obstruction. A negative program does the same thing.

So now you know. You are aware of the subconscious trap, which leads to getting depressed. React. You can regain your love of life. You will reprogram yourself.

SOME IMPORTANT ADVICE

Here are some guidelines before we move on to the formulations themselves.

What kind of inner monologue do you usually have going in your mind? Positive or negative? It must be positive. So observe your own thoughts.

If, like most people, you are subject to temporary periods of depression, increase the frequency of your sessions during those periods. If you experience some kind of setback, accident or other stressful event, I suggest you immediately do an emergency session. You won't solve anything by getting drunk, or by harboring negative thoughts and accusing people of being unfair, mean and so on. Bathe your mind in positive thoughts. Inundate it with the light of your inner sun, both immediately following the unfortunate event and for the next few days, until things get back to normal.

And they will. Life goes on, and things usually aren't as bad as they may first appear. After all, you're alive- that's the important thing. New experiences are awaiting you, marvelous and enriching things are going to happen to you. Turn the page, forget the past and get on with living. The past is only of value for the lessons it teaches us. What counts is today.

TODAY

Yesterday doesn't exist. It's only an illusion in your mind. There is only the present - the joy of being alive here and now. The profound source of your being is happiness, which is beyond all negativity. Complete happiness. Depression is only an illusion. You are happy. You are. Don't be fooled. You are stronger than the circumstances you have to deal with, but you don't realize it. Not yet. You can feel it, you have a presentiment of it. You feel your love of life returning. Soon you will feel it completely. Because you are love and joy.

JOY- HAPPINESS

These are the two words I suggest you concentrate on first and foremost. They will have a marvelous effect. Repeat them. You know them already...

I am the abundance of life

Repeat this phrase and your depression will become a distant memory. Or you can think:

I am becoming a stronger person all the time. I have confidence in life, and I am regaining my love of life. May my joy be with me always. I feel more and more happy. I am in harmony with the flow of life, which rewards me with an abundance of life and happiness.

Or you can use this variation of a formulation you know already, and which is perfectly suited for overcoming feelings of depression:

**Every day, in all ways,
I am becoming stronger and stronger, confident, happy and healthy**

VISUAL VARIATION

You have to create a bank of positive, happy images for yourself that will neutralize the effects of your depressing thoughts. Try to recall as many happy memories as you can. Visualize them in as much detail as possible.

THE 'POSITIVE FRIEND' VARIATION

Visualize your best friend, or a close relative, or even your partner, approaching you, smiling, and saying: 'Congratulations, you handled the situation so well. But you always do. You look wonderful. You're so positive. You look like you're in a great mood. How do you do it?'

In conclusion, remember that any state of depression can be overcome and transformed into an occasion for rejoicing. And the more you practice self- hypnosis, the less likely you are to get depressed, and the less severe your depression will be when and if you do feel down. In time, you'll become completely immunized against the insidious effects of depression. You'll be strong and balanced. And above all, your state of mind will create more and more favorable and fortunate circumstances in your life, so that you'll hardly have occasion to fight off bouts of depression any more. Your mind can do anything.

Happiness is there for the taking. So take it. Now.

MASTER YOUR EMOTIONS

How many times do we hear people say with regret: 'I couldn't control myself.'

Or: 'I should have said something, but I was afraid.' And so on. Of course, there are a whole range of positive emotions such as love, compassion and sympathy. But there are also many negative feelings - anger, fear, hate, envy, jealousy, impatience and so on.

Few people are really aware' of the power of their emotions, both positive and negative. A positive emotion elevates the mind, nourishes you, helps you grow and makes you happy. The most recent scientific studies have shown, beyond the shadow of a doubt, that positive emotions have a direct effect on the body's endocrine system, which plays an essential role in regulating bodily functions.

Negative emotions, especially when they are strongly felt, can disturb glandular and hormonal functions. It's not unusual for women's menstrual cycles to be disturbed by various emotions, like the fear of being pregnant, relationship problems or other kinds of stress.

Negative emotions have an insidious effect on the mind, and can destroy a person's happiness without him or her realizing it. So when we experience feelings of hate for someone, it is really we who are suffering. Because, according to the law of mental causality, every thought is an action, and every action has a reaction.

And one thing is certain - we won't improve relations with anyone, or solve any differences, by harboring thoughts of animosity.

Obviously, the ideal thing would be to think only positive thoughts, and never allow us to be overcome by negative emotions. This is possible, with a little practice. However, to start the process, you must use the law of substitution as soon as a negative emotion enters your mind. Replace the emotion (or thought) with its opposite. For example, you can repeat the words:

PEACE - LOVE

You can also repeat a mantra- a sacred word, or group of words, endowed with a very powerful mystic significance. The mantra I'm going to suggest has been used by millions of people for centuries. It is therefore highly charged with powerful positive vibrations. When you feel inundated by negative emotions, whatever their nature, repeat the mantra: OM NAMA SHIVAYA. The words are Sanskrit, and mean: 'I bow before the power that is in me.' I also recommend it for meditation (repeat it for about 20 minutes) and for your relaxation sessions.

You can also repeat another very ancient mantra, used by sages as the natural mantra for breathing: HAMSA. Say HAM as you inhale, and SA as you exhale.

These mantras are actually suggestions, charged with positive energy. They will help you control your emotions.

Here are some more formulations:

I am able to control my emotions perfectly, under any circumstances. I am mastering my reactions completely. I am becoming more and more positive and fulfilled, in all situations.

VISUAL VARIATION

Imagine yourself in a situation where you are controlling your emotions without difficulty. Visualize an ideal scene. If you are shy with other people, for example, and get flustered and say things you don't want to, imagine yourself completely at ease and full of self-confidence.

If you tend to get angry a lot, visualize a scene where you're at work with a group of colleagues. Nothing they say or do can make you lose your calm. Even unexpected problems do not engender negative emotions in you. Your colleagues and friends appreciate your company, because you are always in perfect control of your negative emotions.

An emotion can kill a person. It can also transform your life. Learn how to neutralize negative emotions, and they will soon be replaced by positive ones.

HOW TO OVERCOME CERTAIN OTHER HABITS

You now understand the real nature of all habits, as well as the fact that you can change them through self-hypnosis. I don't have to repeat the basic principles - you know how to apply them to overcome almost any kind of harmful habit. Here are a few more possible applications, dealing with common problems.

IT'S EASY TO STOP DRINKING

Alcohol is a problem for a lot of people. The difficulty about overcoming the habit is that drinking is an important social pastime. Wherever we go, the first thing we are offered is a drink. In addition, it is hard for an individual to eliminate the influence of alcohol because the body builds up a tolerance (or need) for it on a physiological level.

Of course, there are social drinkers and there are out-and-out alcoholics. There's nothing wrong with having a glass of wine with your meal, or a good brandy afterwards. Problems arise when it becomes impossible (or someone to pass up a drink -when a person no longer chooses when to drink but becomes a slave to alcohol. And alcohol, when consumed too frequently, and especially in excess, is a real poison. It affects the heart, the arteries and, of course the liver. It also affects behavior, often ruining marriages or promising careers.

There's a saying that goes, 'He who has drunk will drink.' Not true, fortunately - for the simple reason that drinking is a habit, a program. And you can change the program like this.

Formulation No. 1: For those who can have the occasional drink, but want to reduce the amount they consume:

I am easily able to control my drinking habit, now I drink only moderate amounts of alcohol. I can easily go for days without drinking. And the less I drink, the better my health is. I am mastering my habits, and my general condition is improving daily. I love my body, and I want to stay healthy for as long as possible. So I take care of it. I drink in moderation. I can go for days without drinking, and I am perfectly happy.

Formulation No. 2: For those who must not touch alcohol at all.

I am giving up alcohol completely. It's easy for me not to drink, and I feel so much better. My body and mind are completely free from the habit of drinking. I am more and more in control of my emotions. I can stop drinking completely, starting today. I am a sober and happy person.

THE 'GOOD FRIEND' VARIATION

Imagine yourself at a party, smiling as you refuse a drink that someone is offering you. 'No, thanks,' you say. 'I don't drink.' You feel perfectly at ease. A friend overhears you and says, 'Well, congratulations! I admire your discipline.

You look much better now that you've stopped drinking. I don't drink either. And I must say, I feel great this way.'

STOP BITING YOUR NAILS!

Nail biting is the perfect example of a compulsive habit. It is usually the result of some kind of anxiety, impatience or frustration, and responds extremely well to treatment through self-hypnosis, as no serious form of dependency is involved.

Here's a formulation:

I don' t feel any need to bite my nails. I can easily get rid of the habit. My hands are starting to look beautiful and elegant, as they should.

For a visual variation, visualize your hands with manicured, elegant nails.

OVERCOMING LAZINESS AND MESSINESS

These two bad habits often go hand in hand. You allow yourself to become messy because you're lazy, and the lack of order in your life makes you even more lazy, both physically and mentally. You let yourself go, and end up in a deplorable state.

Here's a formulation:

All aspects of my life are becoming more and more organized. I am disciplined and confident. I work better, and feel more courageous. I take pleasure in all the little tasks of daily life. I have all the energy I need to do the things I have to do.

Every morning I wake up full of energy, and attack the day with discipline and determination.

Kleptomania

The term 'kleptomania' refers to the habit of compulsive stealing, most of the time against one's own wishes, which is what makes it a 'mania'. The desire to steal is irrepressible. A kleptomaniac is quite different from an ordinary thief. Thieves usually steal to survive - it's the way they make a living, so to speak.

Kleptomaniacs, on the other hand, usually have no need for the things they steal.

The act is impulsive - often the result of a neurosis which, in turn, is the result of a serious inner conflict. Each act of theft reinforces the habit. Here is a formulation to break this embarrassing and harmful habit, which can have terrible consequences on the lives of the people suffering from it.

I feel happy with what I aready have. I am in perfect control of my reactions and impulses, grben I go shopping, I always pay for the things I buy. I can easily control my impulses. I take pleasure in spending money on the things I want. I am a perfectly honest person, and happy to be so.

PUT AN END TO BEDWETTING!

Bedwetting, or enuresis, can be extremely annoying. You have to change the sheets every morning, and wash nightclothes every day. There are a number of methods for curing the disorder, but the simplest is the one I am about to describe.

It usually takes a couple of weeks to work, sometimes even a little longer - but it almost always succeeds.

Children who wet their beds are usually hypersensitive, or have parents who are too demanding. Enuresis is a subconscious way of protesting. We must therefore look to the subconscious to find a cure. This must be done while the child is sleeping. And it's best if the child is not aware of what his or her parents are doing.

If the child wakes up, stop immediately and continue the following night. After the child has fallen asleep, repeat the following formulations about 20 times, in a gentle monotone:

You always ask Mummy when you want to go to the lavatory, and you never make your bed dirty. It's easy for you to stay dry and clean all night long.

If the child is very young, use even simpler words that he or she can easily understand. For example, substitute 'peepee' or 'pooh' for going to the lavatory.

PHOBIAS AND FEARS

Almost everyone suffers from some kind of fear or phobia. That's perfectly normal, and not serious as long as it doesn't prevent us from functioning or make our life miserable. The list of possible phobias and fears is almost endless: fear of lifts, of crowds, heights, of the dark, of dogs and so on.

However, even though there is such an infinite variety of phobias and fears, they all have one thing in common: they are usually linked to some kind of trauma or accident. In addition, they are habits- the result of a program that has been installed in the subconscious. Therefore, a few sessions of well-planned self-hypnosis are usually enough to cure the condition. Sometimes even one session is sufficient.

You can precede the treatment with a little self-analysis - set up a dialogue with your subconscious in order to discover the cause of your trauma, and in turn of your phobia. But this isn't absolutely necessary - the treatment will be effective with or without self-analysis.

I recommend the technique of 'mental cinema', supported by a few verbal formulations, as the best way to cure fears and phobias. So to cure a fear of lifts, visualize yourself calmly entering a lift. You feel very relaxed. If there are any other passengers, you smile at them, and exchange a few pleasantries. Accompany this ideal situation with the following formulation:

I am easily able to take a ride in a lift. I now feel perfectly relaxed whenever I'm in a lift. I am in complete control of my reactions and emotions. I am able to master the situation completely, and I feel calm and relaxed.

Adapt this type of formulation for any type of phobia. Use words that have a calming, relaxing effect, and always refer to the fact that you are in perfect control of your reactions and emotions.

Visualize an ideal situation. In a short time, this ideal scene will become a reality. You will be completely rid of your phobias and fears, whatever they may be.

SUMMARY OF CHAPTER 5

- Making an effort of will is not enough to change a habit. You also have to use the power of your subconscious mind.
- If you want to lose weight:

1. Make a firm decision to lose weight.
2. Establish your ideal weight and set it as a goal.
3. Use a positive formulation.
4. Reinforce the formulation with positive images.

- You can stop smoking in two weeks. Use the formulations and visual techniques described in this chapter.
- Troublesome events are not the real cause of depression. Rather, it is a person's state of mind when such events occur that is responsible. Think, 'I am an abundance of life. There is a solution, and I'm going to find it.' You are stronger than the circumstances around you.
- To control your emotions, think: 'Peace - Love.' Repeat the mantra OM NAMA SHIVAYA, or HAM (as you inhale) and SA (as you exhale). Use positive images and formulations.
- This chapter also includes techniques for dealing with:
- -Drinking too much
- -Nail biting -Laziness and messiness
- -Kleptomania
- -Bedwetting
- -Phobias and fears

6
HOW TO IMPROVE YOUR LOVE LIFE

OVERCOMING YOUR FEAR OF THE OPPOSITE SEX

The greatest obstacle to having a happy love life - as well as one of the most common - is people's fear of the opposite sex and their refusal (often unconscious) to get involved in a relationship. This fear is usually unreasonable and, unfortunately, uncontrollable. The first to deplore it are those who suffer from it.

They know very well that it is stupid to be afraid of the opposite sex. But, as in many other scenarios that you are familiar with by now, it's stronger than they are.

This fear not only exhibits itself in excessive shyness, but also often takes a more subtle and pernicious form. On the outside, people may not seem to be afraid of the opposite sex. They engage in relationships which, to all intents and purposes, appear harmonious and fulfilling. They may date the same person for a long time, or live with someone, or even be married. But deep down, despite themselves, they maintain an underlying fear of their partner that prevents them from being completely happy in their relationships. They are suffering from a mental block.

Another aspect of this fear is especially common among adolescents (and quite naturally so). It is the fear of the unknown, in this case of the first sexual relationship.

But even after being initiated into the pleasures of sex, many people still remain fearful of the opposite gender. Men are just as shy as women. They are afraid of not being worthy. They dare not take the first step. They keep a terribly negative inner monologue going, telling themselves things like, 'She's too beautiful for me.

I'll never be able to please her. I don't have enough class. It'll never work. Why would she want to go out with someone like me?' And so on. This kind of self- deprecatory discourse is obviously harmful.

There are many reasons why people develop a fear of the opposite sex, and they often go back to early childhood. Freud's comments on the subject were full of insight, and included the hypothesis that no one can enter into a successful relationship until their Oedipus complex has been resolved. Being too attached to a mother or father is certainly an obstacle to a successful relationship, and often creates just such a fear of the opposite sex, which is really a way of hiding the guilt associated with incestuous feelings of love for one or the other parent.

Another frequent reason for people's inability to commit themselves and really love someone is a past rejection, and the fear of being rejected, and therefore of suffering, again. Once bitten, twice shy, as the saying goes. Whatever the cause, the various forms of fear of the opposite sex can be overcome through proper reprogramming. These fears are mental and subconscious. They are programs that have been directing our conduct in relationships for years.

Love is the most natural thing in the world. It is your absolute right. When you're shy and don't dare approach someone, or accept an initial invitation, remind yourself that in all likelihood the other person is just as frightened as you are, and for the same irrational reasons. It's all in your head. If you've been rejected in the past, read on. I know it's easier said than done. You may have suffered a lot. But a new relationship can bring you extraordinary joy - who knows? Stop living in the past. And if you've suffered a series of disappointments, do a little self-analysis.

It's not the other person's responsibility. Don't forget that your mind creates the situations you experience. You are probably programmed to fail in love, instead of to fall in love. Your subconscious faithfully adheres to this program and infallibly brings you into contact with those who are likely to make you suffer. And that makes you afraid. But we're going to change all that. You can be the lover you've always dreamed of being, and meet your ideal partner.

Here's a formulation:

I feel better and better in my relationships with the opposite sex. I feel more and more fulfilled in the company of [men or women]. I have harmonious relationships with [men or women]. I'm completely at ease, and many [men or women] find me extremely attractive. I'm more and more confident, and sure of myself around [men or women].

I give love, and receive love, freely
I have the right to be happy with my chosen love

VISUAL VARIATION

Imagine the ideal situation. In a public place you see a man or woman whom you find attractive. You approach that person, feeling confident and sure of yourself.

You smile, and start a conversation. The person smiles back. You offer to buy a drink, or take a walk together. He or she accepts enthusiastically. You feel a marvelous sense of harmony between you, there's already a feeling of budding tenderness. And you find each other very attractive .... You take it from there!

HOW TO LIVE AS A SUCCESSFUL COUPLE AND MAKE LOVE GROW

This is a hard nut to crack, especially in these modern times. It may even be impossible. There are so many divorces, separations, infidelities. And yet there are still a few happy couples around - people who are really happy. In love, happiness is a question of attitude. Love is a state of mind. Of course there's the element of affinity and compatibility between two people. It may sound a little silly, but the best time to prevent a divorce, and other conjugal problems, is before you get married! It's very important to choose the right partner.

If you're single at the moment, I'm going to give you a magic formula for meeting your ideal partner. For 20 days, repeat this formulation 20 times every night:

I am getting closer and closer to meeting my ideal patner, whom I will love deeply, and who will love me deeply in return.

Also, try to compose a profile of the person you'd like to meet. Use the 'blackboard technique' to make a list of qualities you're looking for in a lover or marriage partner. Plant these images in your subconscious mind. It, in turn, will create circumstances in your life that are favorable for fulfilling your desire.

Without knowing exactly how or why, as if by chance, you will soon come across the person you're seeking.

However, you must be sincere in what you want. You also have to be fairly dear about the type of person you're looking for. You may not know it, but this is without a doubt the most difficult part of loving, and the cause of a good proportion of the frustrations and disappointments we experience - you have to make a clear choice. Decide sincerely that you want to love. Most people don't know what the3/expect from love. They don't know what they want. Their expectations are confused, and their love life, being the mirror of those expectations, is also in a state of confusion.

Of course, once you meet the person you think is right for you, life as a couple becomes a lot simpler. You'll always have your little conflicts, but they won't be serious. Life as a couple demands constant adaptation and, above all, an appropriate state of mind. You have to be open to the other person, and allow love to develop. You have to take the initiative and show your love, deliberately and daily. You have to invest in the relationship. If you're in a relationship now and you're having problems, you don't necessarily have to throw in the towel. In my opinion, one of the greatest faults of our time is a tendency to be too impatient, to want things right away.

Repeat this formulation after adapting it to your specific needs:

My relationship with X is becoming more harmonious day by day. We are more fulfilled and happier. We are evolving together, and we complement each other perfectly in more and more ways. I love X, and be/she loves me in return.

Abundantly. I live in a plenitude of love and life. X is love. I am love.

For couples to retain 'that loving feeling', both partners first have to find harmony in themselves, in the depths of their subconscious. The formulation I have just given is extremely effective. It will be sure to help you evolve and become a more loving person.

However, paradoxically enough, improving your relationship may lead to a separation. You asked your subconscious to make you happy in love. Your subconscious knows whether your present partner is right for you or not. You have to trust its guidance and admit that in certain situations separation is not a bad thing, even if it causes nostalgia or regret. Don't forget that it takes two to make a couple. Love is a path that helps you evolve in life. There may be a fork in the path, and the best thing for you both may be to separate. But don't worry - it's always for the best. A new love is waiting to be discovered.

HOW TO OVERCOME IMPOTENCE

The problem of male impotence, so long kept secret, is much more widespread than people believe. It could even be said that all men, at some point or other in their lives, suffer from impotence. Stress, excessive fatigue, alcohol or drug abuse are all causes. What is encouraging is that medical studies have shown that most cases of impotence are of psychological origin. Of course, there can also be physiological reasons, among them the factor of age.

However, rest assured that men can remain sexually active well into old age, as long as they maintain an acceptable level of physical and mental hygiene. Your real sexual organ is your brain, as the saying goes. People who are positive and mentally healthy generally have fulfilling sex lives. And the opposite is also true - psychological problems can lead to impotence. The two are closely linked.

There are a number of forms of male impotence. The most common is an inability to become completely erect. In other cases, men can have an erection but cannot maintain it long enough. Or they lose their erection the moment they attempt penetration (which is the classic example of psychological impotence, since obviously there is nothing wrong with the sexual mechanism, and the problem occurs only at the 'fatal' moment). And finally there's premature ejaculation, which is one of the commonest forms of impotence.

In almost all cases impotence can be cured, quickly and definitively. Subjects can even acquire more sexual vigor than they had before. They can learn to hold back ejaculation at will, effortlessly, and to the great satisfaction of their partners. Every time they make love will seem like the first time. In short, subjects will rediscover their natural erotic nature. All they have to do is change their program.

Impotence is a classic example of a program that is reinforced with every failed attempt to overcome it. Men are haunted by their past failures. Every time they have a new sexual encounter, they become anxious, asking themselves questions like, 'Will I be able to get an erection? Will I be able to hold back long enough?'

And so on.

The answer to these questions is often determined in advance. And, of course, the answer is no. Subjects develop a kind of neurosis about their failure to perform adequately in sexual situations, when all they have to do is reprogram themselves.

Nothing could be simpler. And our studies show that, more often than not, the results are spectacular.

Here's a formulation to repeat:

I can easily have a strong and lasting erection. I am able to satisfy my partner with ease. I ejaculate when I decide to ejaculate. I have perfect control over my ejaculatory reflex. I enjoy making love more and more. I am more and more skilled as a lover, and more and more in love with my partner. I am becoming more potent all the time, and I satisfy my partner fully.

VISUAL VARIATION

The curative power of images cannot be stressed enough in cases of impotence. It is an area where images come easily. You have two choices: either you can draw on your own erotic memories, reliving nights of fulfilling love when you were able to satisfy your partner with ease, and accompany these images with appropriate formulations. Or you can imagine an ideal situation, either with your partner or with any other woman. You undress her, caress her and become fully erect. She is aware of how excited you are, and admires your virility. She makes flattering remarks about your physical attributes. After some skilful and passionate foreplay, you penetrate her. She shudders with pleasure. You remain powerfully erect as long as you wish, retaining your ejaculation until she is satisfied. She feels full of gratitude, as do you. She congratulates you, praising your virility, and telling you what a wonderful lover you are.

FRIGIDITY NEED NO LONGER BE A PROBLEM

Despite the sexual revolution, all is not perfect in the paradise of love. Many women suffer from frigidity - often because of their men, it is true. As the nineteenth-century French author Balzac once said, 'There are no frigid women, only insensitive men.' However, it must be admitted that in many cases women themselves are responsible, at least partially, since they are not able to have an orgasm even when stimulating themselves.

Of course there are numerous causes of frigidity: fear of the male organ, some kind of sexual trauma during childhood, feeling guilty about pleasure, a desire to injure an unfaithful partner and so on. But a common factor in almost all cases is that the woman does not like her body enough - in other words, she has a negative self-image. She does not find herself desirable. Her breasts may be too small, for example, her thighs too large or her hips too heavy. Her self-image is so negative that she feels she has no right to experience pleasure.

In addition, many women are afraid of letting themselves go. They refuse to abandon themselves to their own pleasure, as if there were some kind of danger involved, even though this abandon is the only way to achieve complete satisfaction. Just like impotent men, they are controlled by a negative program and must do some work on themselves. A little self-analysis will often reveal the underlying cause of frigidity.

Here's a formulation to cope with frigidity:

I love my body, and I bare the right to be sexually fulfilled. I find it easier and easier to bare an orgasm. I love my orgasms, and abandon myself completely, in total confidence. I am becoming a sexually fulfilled woman, vibrant and sensual. I can bare orgasms easily, and I can satisfy my partner fully. I love my body, and my partner's body, and I am becoming more and more desirable.

VISUAL VARIATION

Many women have never experienced an orgasm at all. Therefore, they cannot look to their erotic memories for images of fulfillment. If you are one of these women, don't worry. Your imagination will come to your rescue.

Visualize an ideal situation, either with your partner or with some other man. He is a skilful lover, sensitive, passionate and tender. He finds you enormously attractive. You drive him wild, and he makes you crazy with desire. You caress each other until you are both intoxicated with pleasure. Then he penetrates you.

You love the feeling of his penis inside you. You are open, receptive to his every movement. He caresses you skillfully, doing exactly what you like best, and you have a powerful orgasm, abandoning yourself completely to your ecstasy.

Afterwards, your partner is overflowing with praise and gratitude. You have attained sexual harmony and fulfillment together.

HOW TO AWAKEN DESIRE

Sometimes partners, although perfectly functional as far as sex is concerned, allow a kind of routine to set in for one reason or another. And routine is a sure-fire way to extinguish desire. They make love mechanically, because they know it's healthy, not because they really desire each other. The sad thing is that they still love each other, but their absence of desire makes them look elsewhere for satisfaction.

However it is possible to reawaken desire, to regain that original sense of ardor and excitement. If only one of the partners is suffering from a lack of desire, then he or she must replace their negative program with a positive one. Incidentally, routine is not the only reason for an absence of desire. It can also be the result of a kind of apathy, bordering on depression. People sometimes simply lose their lust for life. If both partners have become sexually apathetic, then they should reprogram themselves together.

Here's an appropriate formulation:

I am more and more sexually aroused. My whole body vibrates with desire and love. I am more and desirable, and I find my partner [X] more and more desirable.

I find [him or bet] irresistibly attractive, charming and sensual. My desire grows day by day, and my sexual life is improving in all ways.

In conclusion, I would like to remind you that love and sexual fulfillment are your absolute right in this life. Even if you see couples all around you in conflict and actually breaking up, remember that conjugal happiness is possible. You can be happy in love!

SUMMARY OF CHAPTER 6

- You can overcome your fear of the opposite sex. Think: 'I give and receive love freely. I have the right to be happy with my chosen love.'
- To meet your ideal partner, program your subconscious. Make a sincere decision that yes, you want to love and be loved in return. Rest assured, you will be rewarded.
- You can use the formulations in this chapter to improve your love life. You will also find techniques for overcoming impotence and frigidity and for awakening desire. You can be happy in love!

7
HOW TO DEVELOP YOUR MEMORY, CREATIVITY AND SPORTING ABILITY

THE SECRET OF AN EFFICIENT MEMORY

There's a saying that goes, 'Memory is that faculty of the mind which forgets.'

And forgetting can be a real problem. How many times has your memory failed you, especially when you most need it? It always seems to happen at the worst of times. All schoolchildren and students experience that horrible feeling when you sit down to do an exam and your mind goes blank, even though you revised well enough and thought you knew everything you had to know.

As a matter of fact, you do know, but memory can be capricious. The more you dig through your gray matter, the more elusive the information you are looking for becomes. Actually, this is one of the ways that the 'law of inverse effect' formulated by Emile Coué works: the more you want to remember something, the harder it is to find.

When an actor has a memory lapse, when a student's mind goes blank during an exam, when a speaker can't remember what he wanted to say in front of an audience, in all these instances the person's imagination (or subconscious mind) takes over their will (or conscious mind). The dominant message being communicated by the subconscious (and therefore its dominant program) is one of failure - the person will not succeed. This creates the mental block - in this case a loss of memory.

And yet these people know what they are unable to remember. As soon as the student steps out of the examination room, all the information he forgot floods back into his mind, effortlessly. But unfortunately it's too late. Likewise the actor knows his role by heart. He's already played it dozens of times, without making any mistakes at all.

All memories are stored in the subconscious: absolutely everything. This should be of great interest to those who would like to improve their power of recall. To do so you have to retain, or maintain access to, your inner memory - your subconscious. Remember that everyone has this excellent, perfect memory hidden in his or her subconscious. It contains every book you have ever read, line for line; all your dreams, all your thoughts, every word ever spoken to you, all the impressions you have, all your feelings; absolutely everything.

Some people have amazing memories. They can recall entire pages of a book after reading it only once, or whole columns of numbers at a glance. Mozart is an illustrious example. His memory for music was phenomenal. He almost always composed in his head, without the help of an instrument. He would retain whole symphonies and then transcribe them in one draft, with no mistakes. In Mozart's day it was forbidden to write music in a church. On one occasion, the young composer heard a mass that he found particularly moving. It lasted two hours. As soon as the service was over, Mozart went home and transcribed the entire piece, note for note, without a single error.

There are many examples throughout history of people with unbelievable powers of recall. You may even know someone personally who has an amazing memory.

What secret do these people possess? It's instant and continual access to their sub-conscious mind with its perfect memory.

Picture the subconscious as being a kind of mental filing cabinet. Each file in each drawer contains specific information. People endowed with a prodigious memory can open any of these drawers, any time they wish.

So you see just how useful self-hypnosis can be for improving your memory, since it is the key to the subconscious. The first thing it will do, if you follow the instructions in this chapter, is to eliminate those annoying memory lapses which almost always occur at the least opportune moment. It would be presumptuous for me to assure you that you will acquire an infallible memory overnight; nevertheless I know you will be surprised at how quickly you progress.

THE MANY ADVANTAGES OF HAVING A GREAT MEMORY

Your efficiency at work will vastly improve. You'll be able to remember the information in your files better and quote the right statistic at the right time. You'll never be at a loss for words, always spontaneously coming up with just the right phrase. When you have to write something, you'll do it more easily and more precisely.

Your level of comprehension and capacity for analysis will improve at the same time. Because the fact is that all intellectual activity depends on memory. Without memory it is impossible to reason, to calculate, to imagine. Improving your memory will also improve your intellectual abilities. And it works both ways.

Better comprehension allows you to memorize things more easily. So you come out a winner in both senses.

Now let's take a look at the techniques. Here's a formulation to repeat:

My memory is improving in all areas of my life. Starting today, I can easily retain everything I need to know, under any circumstances and in any location. My memory is becoming more and more precise and reliable. I absorb all the information I need to carry on with my daily activities more and more easily. My memory is making daily progress and will soon become perfectly efficient. I am in fall control of my memory in all situations.

And here's one for learning a specific subject:

I can easily learn [Spanish], and my memory absorbs the words of the language with increasing facility. I understand Spanish better and better, and I can speak it with ease. My memory of Spanish is improving daily. Learning Spanish is child's play for me.

THE 'FRIEND' TECHNIQUE

Visualize a friend approaching you, smiling. They ask you for some information, for example an important historical date they can't remember. You supply the information, effortlessly. Your friend says, 'Wow, what an amazing memory you have! You should be proud of yourself. You can remember dates, events, statistics, thoughts, what people say to you, what you read ....

You really have a fantastic memory. I envy you...' and so on.

VISUAL VARIATION

One of the best exercises for improving your memory, as well as your concentration (the two go hand in hand), is based on adding numbers. Visualize a large blackboard (as explained earlier, the exercise is still effective even if you can't actually see the blackboard, and the writing on it, in your mind). Imagine yourself holding a piece of white chalk and writing a very large number 1 on the blackboard. Then imagine that you erase the number slowly. You're in no hurry.

You feel perfectly relaxed.

Next you write the number 2. The exercise consists of adding each number you write to the one preceding it. Therefore you start with 1+2=3.

Now erase the 1 and visualize the number 3. The last two numbers are 2 and 3.

Add them up again: 2+3=5.

Erase the 2 and visualize the number 5. Add it to the preceding number: 3 +5 = 8.

Visualize the number 8, and so on, continuing with 13, 21, 34, etc.

After each operation you erase the previous number before adding again.

Continue until you're tired. You'll see that the exercise becomes easier with each session, and you'll be able to go farther and farther. You'll soon be doing it for several minutes at a time. The effects are surprising. Your memory and concentration will improve tremendously. And you'll start seeing results in just a few days.

LEARN WHILE YOU SLEEP!

One of the most amazing things you can do with self-hypnosis is to learn while you sleep. It's a marvelous technique, especially in emergency situations. Say you have to study some material fast for an exam. Or you're an actor, and you're asked to stand in for someone who is ill. You only have two days to learn the role.

Unfortunately, you have an important meeting the next morning and a lot of shopping to do besides. Well, learn your lines while you sleep!

A word of caution: It's best to reserve this technique for exceptional situations.

Don't abuse it.

Now here's the method. Speak what you want to learn into a tape recorder. Place the machine close to your bed. You start by listening to the tape while you're awake, before you close your eyes. Then lower the sound so that it won't wake you up. Get someone to come in and start the tape an hour later (or purchase an electronic timer to turn the machine on automatically). Also, before falling asleep, make the following suggestions to yourself:

Soon I will be deeply asleep. And yet I will easily be able to hear what I recorded, and I will memorize it effortlessly without waking up. I'll learn the recorded text easily, in total relaxation and calm.

When you wake up, listen to the tape again, before you get out of bed.

CONCENTRATION: THE KEY TO SUCCESS

If I had to identify a common factor, a characteristic typical of all successful people, I would choose- aside from positive thinking, of course - the ability to concentrate on a specific activity. It doesn't matter what kind of work you do - there are no exceptions. You may be in business, you may be an artist, a politician, an athlete or a movie producer. All successful people, all those who have made a mark in their respective fields, know how to concentrate.

In cases of exceptional success, where persons attain a kind of glory or mythical status in their chosen field, a kind of complete single-mindedness, an ability to concentrate totally on a single idea, can always be observed. These people are tenacious and incredibly persevering. They direct all their energy, all their strength, heart and soul towards one clearly defined goal.

Constant and well-directed concentration in any sphere of activity will always produce results. Unfortunately, people who are unable to concentrate, who suffer from a 'grasshopper' state of mind, will rarely achieve success. And there are lots of them. How many times have you heard someone say, 'I just can't concentrate. I always get distracted. I can't spend more than five minutes on the same subject...' and so on.

It's a very common complaint. And being able to concentrate doesn't only affect your professional life or your ability to study at school or college. It also affects your inner life, your psychology and your general behavior. Because people who can't concentrate enough to read a magazine article, or work out a simple math equation, are also unable to concentrate on their own lives. Such people are usually unable to solve their own problems: they can't see things clearly.

Concentrating means sorting things out, bringing them into the light of day and finding solutions. It is the ability to fix your mind on a specific object for a given period of time, to the point where you forget the exterior world and eliminate all distractions.

When I was young I lived in a place where the summers were hot and wet.

During the long summer holidays I would spend sultry, rainy days with a friend, playing cards. A waste of time, you say? Not at all. I found that I was so absorbed in the game that I didn't mind the heat and the rain at all. I was, in fact, anaesthetized. My body was insensitive to the heat. I didn't think about it at all.

I related this little anecdote to show you how powerful concentration can be. If you are unable to concentrate, don't worry. Concentration is a faculty that can be developed through training. It's just like a muscle: the more you exercise it, the stronger it becomes. And it's easy to improve your concentration, especially with the exercise I am going to show you. It's extremely effective. It will not only improve your mental concentration - it will literally change your life.

This is due to the fact that, as you become a concentrated person, you acquire what is commonly called 'presence'. You are much more aware of what goes on in the present moment. And this, in turn, endows you with a magnetic personality.

You become an important person, a person to be reckoned with. People will listen to what you have to say. They'll stop interrupting you. They'll find you irresistibly attractive, and use you as a measure of their own abilities.

In addition, you'll feel a lot more positive towards the people around you. You'll like them more, since your new found ability to concentrate will allow you to see them as they really are. You'll be aware of their qualities and eccentricities, in a new and special way. You'll be able to look at someone and say to yourself, 'Hm, so that's what she's really like ....'

If you already know the person, it will be like seeing him Or her through new eyes, for the very first time. If you're meeting the person for the first time, you'll feel as if you know exactly who you're dealing with straight away. You'll intuitively know what people are really thinking when they speak, as if you could read their minds. People won't be able to lie to you without your knowing it. What an advantage this can be, both at work and in life in general.

As for personal problems, the more you learn to concentrate, the easier it will be to solve them. Life is, in a sense, like a puzzle. What may have seemed unsolvable before - precisely because you lacked the ability to concentrate sufficiently- will become child's play now. Solutions will jump out at you, in the clear light of your concentrated mind. You'll be like Picasso, who once said, 'I don't seek, I find.'

AN INCREDIBLY POWERFUL EXERCISE

Now for the exercise itself. It's very simple, as you will see. But don't be fooled by its simplicity - the results are no less spectacular. It's also a very old exercise, which has been practiced by millions of people. I have already described a variation in the section on inducing the state of self-hypnosis. The exercise consists of concentrating on a single point.

Draw a small circle on the ground in front of you or on the wall (alternatively use a self-adhesive sticker). Stare at this point, without frowning or straining your eyes.

Your face should remain perfectly relaxed. Don't blink (at least try to reduce the number of times you blink). At first you may feel some itching or slight burning around your eyes, or they may start running. Don't worry - the exercise is very good for you - it actually improves vision and adds sparkle to your eyes, which will give you a magnetic gaze that will irresistibly attract people to you.

Start by staring at the point for one minute. Gradually increase the length of time, up to a limit of about 20 minutes. But don't force yourself- take your time. While staring at the point you can concentrate on your breathing, or repeat one of the mantras I've already given you: OM NAMA SHIVAYA or HAMSA.

Mentally repeating these mantras is in itself an extremely powerful exercise in concentration. If the exercise of staring at a fixed point doesn't appeal to you, you can repeat a mantra instead. Close your eyes when doing this. And of course, combining the two exercises- staring at a point and repeating a mantra-will provide excellent results.

Do the exercise at least once a day. The best time is in the morning. Even doing it for only five or ten minutes a day, you'll end up saving yourself an enormous amount of time. Your thoughts will have direction, your powers of reasoning will improve, your mind will be clear and capable of profound reflection. You'll be able to think quickly and precisely. And you will discover a special kind of pleasure in being completely present and aware of what you are doing. In other words, you'll live more intensely, in the present moment, absorbed in the here and now, unfettered by the past, not worried about the future, and yet on the road to spectacular success. Concentration is the key.

HOW TO BE CREATIVE AND INSPIRED

Many of us believe that creativity is some kind of natural, heaven-sent gift, that people are born with talent, or with exceptional creativity, or even with genius. It is true that certain people are really endowed with exceptional talent. But many of the people whom we consider 'naturally' creative had to learn to be that way. They developed their creativity simply by relying on the power of their subconscious, and by gaining access to its inexhaustible source of ideas. There are a host of examples.

Did you know, for example, that the famous musician Rachmaninov composed his celebrated Second Piano Concerto while undergoing hypnotic therapy to cure him of chronic depression (the result of the unfavorable criticism his previous works had received) and to stimulate his creativity? He was so pleased with the result that he dedicated the concerto to his hypnotist!

Even the great Michelangelo, a universal symbol of creativity, used the power of the subconscious to help him in his work. The following anecdote proves the point: 'One day, while painting in the Vatican, a group of cardinals found him sleeping on his scaffold. They drew his attention to the fact, upon which he replied, "I get more work done while asleep than when I'm awake." In his sleep, he saw all the scenes he would later paint, in the exact colors he was to use.'

Besides Michelangelo a considerable number of painters, writers and musicians have relied on sleep - that is, their subconscious - for inspiration. When the British author Robert Louis Stevenson found himself in financial difficulties he would ask his subconscious for an idea for a commercial book-one that would become a bestseller. Invariably his subconscious would give him the answer. He would wake up in the morning 'inspired' with the new idea he needed.

INSPIRATION CAN BE PROGRAMMED

In fact, inspiration is not some kind of mysterious or magical process, as we are led to believe. Rather, it is an ability to access the subconscious mind, the repository of ideas and images necessary for all creation. Getting inspired is simple. Anyone can do it. Anyone can develop his or her creativity. Of course I'm not saying that you can become another Chopin or Picasso overnight. But you will certainly develop your own creative potential, which already exists in a latent state inside you. You'll be more creative, not only at work but also in your pastimes, in your relationships and in your life in general. You'll be more spontaneous and more imaginative. And a touch of madness or fantasy is a necessary element for happiness in this life. You can acquire it. Your life will become a game, a work of art that you keep on perfecting, touch by touch.

Yes, becoming creative and inspired is simple. All you need is the right program.

I suggest two exercises. Use the first when you have a specific problem, for example when you're looking for an idea to write about, or the solution to a problem, or a concept for some business project (or ways to develop an existing business) and so on. Hold a dialogue with your subconscious: ask it for an answer.

My sibconscient is helping me find the solution I'm looking for. I will get the response I need easily. What is the best way to [formulate your problem]...?

The second method is more general, and will improve your overall creativity:

I am more and more creative and inspired in all areas of my life. I have access to an abundance of ideas, and solutions to all kinds of problems, because I can draw on the inexhaustible source of my subconscious.

I might add in passing that just practicing relaxation will make you more creative since, whenever you enter the alpha state, you also enter into contact with your subconscious and all its treasures.

HOW TO DEVELOP YOUR ATHLETIC ABILITY

Athletic prowess is not uniquely innate, contrary to what many people think.

Certainly some people are born more gifted than others. Heredity is a factor, and not everyone can become a world champion. Nevertheless, anyone can develop their physical abilities, whatever natural gifts they happen to possess. And this is for a very simple reason: muscles are controlled by the subconscious.

Tennis, bowling, golf and most other sports depend to a great degree on technique and concentration. Incidentally, by practicing the concentration exercises described in the previous sections you will also considerably improve your performance in whatever sport you do. Technique and concentration are essential, and so is relaxation, because well-coordinated movements and full exploitation of your muscle power are not possible unless you are relaxed.

In competitive sport, nerves count for a lot, since there is often an enormous amount of tension involved. All great champions, whatever their discipline, agree that at a certain high level of competition sport becomes a kind of 'mind game'.

You win or lose in your head, before you do so on the playing field. And it's in your mind - in your subconscious mind - that you must first acquire the skills you need.

Not everyone plays to win, of course. Many people do not enjoy competing.

They play sports to relax, to stay in shape, to meet people. And those are perfectly legitimate reasons. However, everyone does like to excel, or at least be good enough to make the game interesting. Nothing could be more natural. We take pleasure in doing things well.

INFALLIBLE METHODS FOR IMPROVING YOUR ATHLETIC ABILITY

These methods are used the world over by Olympic teams from different countries, and by champions of all nationalities and disciplines. The results are spectacular. They can also work for you, even if you only take part in a sport for the fun of it; they will improve your performance substantially.

The basis of these methods is nothing more than a variation of the 'mental cinema' technique I have already described. We can call them 'imaginary training sessions'. You perform the activity in your mind, imagining every move. Take tennis, for example. You visualize yourself on the court, completely relaxed. Your muscles respond perfectly to your commands. Your reflexes are sharp. Your volleys are precise and executed with ease. All your shots are fluid and accurate - serve, smash, lob, backhand and so on.

If you're involved in competitive sports and play to win, modify the exercise a little. Visualize yourself winning point after point. You have a powerful serve, and serve ace after ace. Your opponent is devastated, hardly able to make a shot. And you take advantage of every opportunity, smashing to the backcourt, lobbing when he or she advances to the net - all perfectly executed. You can even visualize yourself accepting the trophy, while the crowd applauds and you smile and bow, triumphant.

You see, it's simple. And I should add that in order to win, it is essential to do this kind of mental exercise. Remember what we said about the importance of a positive self-image. To win, your self-image must be that of a winner. It is an absolutely essential condition. And to play well, you have to program your sub- conscious. Athletes call it 'muscular memory' - for a movement to be executed perfectly, it must come from the subconscious and not the conscious mind. This is what makes a movement really natural and effective. It is the only way to play a game really well, especially if a lot of strength and skill is required.

Golf is another example. There are so many details to think about to make a perfect shot that if you had to think about them all consciously you couldn't handle it - the operation is too complex. The only way to make a good shot is to rely on your subconscious.

Accompany your 'mental cinema' sessions with appropriate verbal formulations.

Tennis

I'm playing tennis with more and more facility. I execute all my shots with increasing success. Tennis is becoming an easy sport for me. I am improving day by day. I win more and more matches.

Golf

My golf technique is improving day by day. I hit the ball with power and precision, in any situation. My swing is smooth and efficient. My iron shots are as good as my woods, and I'm baying a lot of success with putting. Golf is becoming easy for me. My handicap is dropping, and I'm playing a lot better without making any extra effort.

Archery

I am a perfectly relaxed archer. My reflexes are getting faster and sharper. I bit the target consistently and easily. Shot after shot. All aspects of my skill are improving. My eyesight and my reflexes are excellent. Archery is easy for me.

Bowling

My bowling technique is improving day by day. My approach is smooth and relaxed. I launch the wood with more and more precision. I have perfect control and can make any throw I want. I am becoming a winner in tournaments. My score improves every time I play. Bowling is easy for me.

These are only four examples out of a host of other possibilities. Adapt the formulations to your own sport. You know how to do that by now. And you'll be amazed by the results. Don't forget to do repeated visualizations as well.

Programming your subconscious to win, or at least to improve your game, will soon lead to considerable progress - even if your style isn't exactly classic and even if you don't have an athletic physique. And remember, you don't need to know how the subconscious produce results. All you need to know is that it does work. That's what counts. So have fun, and good luck!

SUMMARY OF CHAPTER 7

- The subconscious remembers everything. To have a prodigious memory, all you have to do is program your mind through self-hypnosis.
- You can learn while sleeping. Tape-record the formulation provided in this chapter and listen to it, along with the text you need to learn, before going to sleep. Do so again an hour after you fall asleep. When you wake up, you'll remember everything easily.
- Concentration is the key to success. To develop your concentration, use the technique of concentrating on a fixed point.
- Program yourself to be inspired and creative. Develop your athletic abilities through positive formulations and image training.

8

CHOOSING SUCCESS, NOT FAILURE

LEARN TO MOTIVATE YOURSELF FOR SUCCESS

You now possess a powerful tool for success - self-hypnosis. But you mustn't be afraid to motivate yourself for success. You have to believe sincerely that you can be successful. And you have to make a firm decision. You have to choose to succeed.

This may sound a little banal, but it isn't. You may think that everyone wants success, since it's the most obvious kind of ambition there is. But unfortunately, that's just not true. Many people have developed a personality geared to failure.

They are losers, plain and simple. Luck never seems to be on their side. They encounter one problem after another. And, of course, they never stop complaining about their lot in life. Because in fact what these people really want is failure.

Even though they may say they want to succeed, their subconscious mind is pro- grammed for failure. And it carries out its program to the end. If you are one of these people, you must react- not tomorrow, but today!

Of course, we can't always come out a winner (and failure can be very instructive). But if you fail more often than you succeed, stop for a moment and ask yourself this question: Do you, by chance, happen to have a personality programmed for failure? If the answer is yes, you can change it. In fact, you're already well on your way to changing it, since you've taken the trouble to read this book and, I hope, have been applying some of the techniques it suggests.

If you're already successful, you can be even more so. There is no limit to success. Your only limitation, as we've already seen -and it's the strongest kind of limitation there is - is your own mind. As you break through your mental limitations, you break through the limits of your success. Because really there are no limits. Think big and you'll become big. It works every time.

And above all, set goals for yourself. This is essential. The power of having well- defined goals is enormous. Without goals, you don't know where you are going and you don't know where to begin. All your efforts are dispersed and lacking in consistency. Set goals and objectives for yourself, and you will attain them. You'll go beyond them.

There are two kinds of goals you have to establish: long-term and short-term.

They give all your efforts direction and meaning. Start with simple goals that are easily attainable. Be persevering. Don't drop an objective the first time you run up against an obstacle. Your initial victories, although on a small scale, will encourage you to strive for higher objectives and reinforce your new personality, which is being programmed for success.

I will persevere until I am successful

You should be continually impregnating your mind with the idea of success.

Don't let any doubts cloud your sense of purpose. You can succeed. You will succeed. You have everything you need, even if you are not fully aware of it yet.

You have immense potential - the power of your subconscious is yours for the asking.

Now that you have been initiated into the techniques of self-hypnosis, you are one of the fortunate elect. You're already way ahead of other people who have no inkling of the method and its amazing effects. Eliminate all thoughts of failure from your mind. Don't allow the idea of failure to penetrate your subconscious. If your mind refuses to entertain any thoughts of failure, you will never experience failure.

Treat everything that happens to you as a learning process that is leading you towards success. If you encounter an obstacle, try and discover how it's positive - what it can teach you. You'll soon become the winner you really are.

SUCCESS - WEALTH

Repeat these two words constantly. And:

I am more and more successful in everything I do. I am able to achieve my objectives with increasing ease. I am becoming a successful person. Life is good to me. Everything I do succeed. More and more, I experience success after success.

HOW TO HAVE AS MUCH MONEY AS YOU WANT

Financial security is usually an important part of success. Whether you like it or not, having money makes life easier. It's more than a status symbol - it's an instrument. Many people have false ideas about money. They believe they'll never have any, that they were born to mediocrity. It's this kind of conviction that keeps them below the poverty line. Because all the evidence shows that people who are persuaded they will always be poor will probably remain so for the rest of their lives.

In fact, it's not as hard as you may think to become rich, or at least financially comfortable. You can even have as much money as you need. Once again, it all depends on your state of mind.

Real wealth is a state of mind. If you live with the dominant idea of privation and poverty, you will be poor. If you live with the idea of abundance and good fortune, even if your present financial situation is difficult, you will become wealthy. Your subconscious will obey, and in one way or another, without your understanding exactly how it works, will create circumstances favorable for your financial gain.

Money will come to you as if attracted by a magnet. You won't have to spend your time figuring out how to make ends meet at the end of the month.

You can acquire the lifestyle you've always dreamed of having. An interesting job, a luxurious house, a smarter car, frequent trips abroad... you can have it all.

Plant the seeds of wealth in your mind. Don't be afraid to dream a little. But dream scientifically, as you have learnt to do in this book. Reality will soon take the shape of your dreams. Remember these formulations:

SUCCESS – WEALTH
I am abundance
Every dollar I spend comes back to me, multiplied a hundredfold
I earn more money than I spend
I find security in myself
I have the right to be lucky and rich

Yes, being rich is your absolute right. Think money! This doesn't mean you have to become avaricious or completely materialistic. When you have all the money you need, you hardly think about it. You don't worry and think negative thoughts all the time. The law of life is the law of abundance. But most people choose to ignore it, or believe that the opposite is true - that life is hardship and misery.

Thanks to the power of your subconscious, you can enter the positive flow of life, the flow of wealth and happiness, this very day!

HOW TO STAY YOUNG AND LIVE LONGER

Real youth is a state of mind. Some people are already old at the age of 20, while others look incredibly good and have amazing energy even at a ripe old age. The secret of staying eternally young is to flow with the current of real life by opening the gates of your subconscious. You now know how to do this. Society has created stereotypes for people of all ages, predicting how we should behave, especially when we reach retirement age. Don't be concerned with these artificial barriers.

You can retire whenever you like, and not when society tells you to. In fact, you don't ever have to retire, because you can stay active and interested in the events and people around you in all ways your whole life long - intellectually, physically, spiritually, sexually and artistically. Think young and you'll stay young. You can add years to your life and, more importantly, life to your years.

Why do you have to consider yourself old at the age of 60? Because everybody thinks that way. Because statistics have shown that

Don't pay any attention to these kinds of prejudiced attitudes. Did you know that the Hunza, a small tribe living in the Himalayas of northern India, can boast a number of centenarians who are still vigorous and active, and even a few members who have reached the venerable old age of 125. And they're in perfect health! They don't know what retirement is. It doesn't exist. Their age categories are completely different. Hunzas become adults at the age of 60, at which point their years of maturity, instead of retirement, begin.

You too can live a very long and healthy life. Repeat these formulations, and visualize your body as being young, strong and healthy.

My body is becoming stronger and more vigorous. I am regaining [or maintaining] full control of all my faculties. My hearing, eyesight and memory are more and more effective and healthy. My face looks younger day by day. And I am getting more attractive all the time. I feel younger and younger, more and more relaxed, healthier and healthier. I am regaining my enthusiasm and the curiosity of my youth. Youth. Youth. I have more and more energy, more and more creativity. I am young in body and in mind.

The real fountain of youth is in your mind, your subconscious mind, which does not grow older. It is eternally young. Become its ally, and it will reward you by keeping you young and protecting you from the vicissitudes of old age.

LEARN TO ENJOY LIFE

Life is the most extraordinary gift you can receive. Don't forget that. Take full advantage of life. Every day, every hour, every minute is precious. Don't waste your time being unhappy. Change your state of mind, and you will change your life. It may be hard at first- our old negative habits can be very resistant. But you can be certain you will win in the end. And the winner's prize is life. You will be triumphant.

Take the time to enjoy life. Live each day as if it were your last-with intensity.

Eliminate useless things that are simply a waste of time. Learn to love everything you do. Don't accept boredom as your lot in life. Don't do what you don't want to do (at least not for too long). Being bored or stuck in a job you hate is a complete waste of time. Ask your subconscious for a solution, and it will be revealed to you.

By entering the current of life, you learn to profit fully from every moment. You will live intensely. Every day of your life will become a marvelous adventure.

SUMMARY OF CHAPTER 8

- Motivate yourself, and persevere until you achieve success. If you don't let any thoughts of failure lodge in your mind, you won't ever fail. Treat everything that happens to you as a kind of learning process that is leading you to success. Look for the positive aspects in the things that happen to you, even if they appear to be negative.
- Wealth is first and foremost a state of mind. Use the

formulations in this chapter to get luck and good fortune on your side.
- To live long and stay healthy, program your subconscious and learn how to enjoy life. Live each day as if it were your last.

YOU CAN DO ANYTHING

AN ANCIENT HINDU LEGEND

There's an ancient Hindu legend told in India.

There was a time when all men were gods. But they so abused their divinity that

Brahma, the supreme creator, decided to deprive them of their divine power, and hide it in a place where it would be impossible to find. The problem was to find a suitable hiding place.

When the minor gods were called to a meeting to resolve the problem, they made the following proposition: Hide the power of divinity somewhere in the earth. But

Brahma refused, saying, 'No, it's too easy. Someone will dig into the earth and find it.'

So the gods replied, 'In that case, hide it in the depths of the ocean.'

But Brahma refused once again, saying, 'No, because sooner or later people will explore all the regions of the ocean. They will surely find it and bring it back to the surface.'

So the gods concluded that they were not able to find a place on land or in the sea where the power of divinity would be safe from man.

Then Brahma said, 'Here's what we'll do with the power of divinity: we'll hide it in the very depths of man himself, because that is the only place he will never think of looking.'

Since that time man has explored the surface of the earth and the ocean depths, looking for something that can be found only in himself.

The hiding place, of course, is your subconscious mind. Now you know. You know that with this omnipotent ally you can do anything. Absolutely anything.

Everything you ever dreamed of can be yours.

Dreaming is your right, and what you desire is yours for the taking: love, success, wealth, health, happiness. You can now become the person you've always dreamed of being. In fact, you already are that person - if you think you are and believe it in the depths of your mind. All you have to do is let your real personality reveal itself. A rebirth is awaiting you. Today.

A spectacular new life lies in store for you. Because life is a state of mind. You are the product of your thoughts. Don't limit your thoughts. The power of thought can accomplish anything.

YOU CAN ACCOMPLISH ANYTHING

APPENDIX

GET TO WORK NOW!

Write these words and phrases on small cards and put them in your wallet, or any other place you're likely to see them often. You can also meditate on them during your sessions of self-hypnosis. Concentrate on the black dots to use the subliminal effect.

SUCCESS

HEALTH

RELAXATION

CONFIDENCE

CALM

JOY

LOVE

Every day, in all ways, I am getting better and better

APPENDIX

It works!

Today I start a new life

Day by day, in every way, I am more and more confident

I have confidence in myself, in others and in life

My personality is becoming more and more MAGNETIC

I can influence the people around me in any way I choose

STRENGTH

I love my body

I have the power to heal myself

I have more and more energy and strength

HAPPINESS

I am abundance

TODAY

PEACE

I am becoming more and more creative

I will persevere until I achieve success

I find security in myself

I have the right to good fortune and wealth

I can do anything

ALSO BY CHRISTIAN H. GODEFROY

Mind Dynamics (free)

Your Personal Passport to Success: How to Get Where You Want to Be

The outstanding negotiator

How to cope with difficult people with Louis Robert

Complete Time Management System

How to write letters that sell with copywriting : Copywriting Techniques for Achieving Success

www.ingramcontent.com/pod-product-compliance
Lightning Source LLC
LaVergne TN
LVHW012043070526
838202LV00056B/5580